Living in Color

Living in Color

What's Funny About Me

TOMMY DAVIDSON

with Tom Teicholz

KENSINGTON BOOKS

www.kensingtonbooks.com

KENSINGTON BOOKS are published by

Kensington Publishing Corp.
119 West 40th Street
New York, NY 10018

All Kensington titles, imprints, and distributed lines are available at special quantity discounts for bulk purchases for sales promotion, premiums, fund-raising, educational, or institutional use.

Special book excerpts or customized printings can also be created to fit specific needs. For details, write or phone the office of the Kensington Special Sales Manager: Attn. Special Sales Department. Kensington Publishing Corp., 119 West 40th Street, New York, NY 10018. Phone: 1-800-221-2647.

Library of Congress Card Catalogue Number: 2019950885

ISBN-13: 978-1-4967-1294-3
ISBN-10: 1-4967-1294-3
First Kensington Hardcover Edition: February 2020

ISBN-13: 978-1-4967-1297-4 (ebook)
ISBN-10: 1-4967-1297-8 (ebook)

10 9 8 7 6 5 4 3 2 1

Printed in the United States of America

To the memory of the Four Musketeers, my family unit growing up, my bloodline, my lifeline: my mother, Barbara Jean, and brother, Michael, and my sister, Beryle, who defined me

To Amanda, who keeps it real and makes it all worthwhile, and for my children, who are my greatest accomplishments

Foreword

I first met Tommy in Chicago at my annual Athletes Against Drugs golf tournament where he performed at the dinner gala. He was then and is now the most talented comedian I have ever seen. We got a chance to spend time together, and my immediate impression of him was that his potential for helping people and impacting their lives went far beyond his performance on stage.

Living in Color is a great read. Once you pick this book up, you do not want to put it down. Tommy's memoir is a journey of someone looking for love and realizing that nobody has a monopoly on it. Love comes in all forms, shapes, sizes, and colors. Tommy first found it with his adopted mom as she helped him realize his gifts, talents, and abilities.

He now shares all of that with us and the world. Tommy Davidson is fortunate to have the strength, resilience, and determination to overcome any obstacle. In fact, he has seen it all on every level. This opportunity is rare and a blessing. Most people are just surviving, doing the same things over and over every day, with little time left to devote to self-mastery and self-actualization. The freedom Tommy has always looked for in his day-to-day battles and resulting victories comes and goes. I can tell from this book that he has the desire and determination to truly find out who he really is and that his full potential is beginning to emerge so, that one day he'll begin to say those beautiful words: "Free at last, free at last, thank God almighty, I am free at last."

—Stedman Graham

Introduction

People ask me all the time about race in America: "Is Trump a racist? Is America becoming more racist?" They want to know what I have to say about race today.

What I tell them is: "Why you asking me? Ask yourself."

What I've learned is that most white people only see me as black. They can't see that a white family raised me; they don't know the story of my mother, my grandparents, my father, brother, and sister. With them, I saw the world that white people see.

When I am performing in a club where the audience is mostly African-American, they see me as black and I can push the black gas pedal down hard, if I choose to, because I understand their sensibility. It is my understanding of both black and white audiences that makes my act.

Seeing the world through the prism of black and white is a talent I have—but it is not how I experience the world. I am part of the family of man. Just one member of the human family. When I'm with friends, family, other people in recovery, and when I'm onstage or performing, then I'm just me. I'm not a color. How I was raised and how I tried to raise my children—in a loving, compassionate, kind, and virtuous home—these traits have no color. Truth, ethics, morals, these are not white or black traits.

To me, "black" is not a color. It's a cultural phenomenon. I have deep respect for all that African Americans have contributed to this country, and to the world.

Onstage I talk honestly about the way white people behave—like what it's like to be standing on a line, waiting at an IHOP, that's when white women take charge. White women speak up for the group. White women are like human rights advocates. White women aren't racist. I'll tell you why I say that: They are experts at defending young black mothers. They want *justice*. They'll go crazy if there's a pregnant black woman with a toddler waiting too long on line. They'll start talking out loud, saying, "We are waiting here! Is anyone here?" She'll say, "That baby's about to pop. Get this kid some pancakes." That's white women to the rescue!

Everyone will nod and laugh because I'm talking about our common humanity. These are the things I've noticed and that we all know, but until I've pointed them out, you never put it together. In my act, I talk about how when black men fight with their friends, they are angry. But when white men fight with their friends, it's as if they like them even more. White men, I like to say, are "emotionally ambidextrous." They can be friends and angry all at the same time.

Like the way frat boys talk to each other, making criticisms seem like terms of affection: "Dude! What the fuck! You are a fucking cretin, man. You are the worst!" For them, that's a term of endearment. They're best friends after that.

But if one black dude says any of that to another brother, he better start running. It gets real dark with us, real fast.

We don't like getting mad. But if I say, "I told you, stop that bullshit, Andre. I ain't going to tell you no mother-fuckin' mo'," there'd be nothing funny about that.

For me, my comedy, my art, my life, is not about putting people down, it's about bringing people together. Finding what we all know, but don't always say.

What was so special about *In Living Color* was that when people saw that the majority of the cast was African-American, they thought it was going to be a black show. But it wasn't. It was about the human family.

In Living Color was the first show of a postracial hip-hop nation. And I'm not sure if there's been another one since.

If you take the long view of history, the story of the human family is not a white story, or a black story, or a yellow story, or a red story, or whatever skin tone you want to talk about. There were African kings, civilizations, and empires long before Anglo-Saxons became civilized.

I'm very proud of my heritage and feel fortunate to be part African in every respect of its amazing, magnificent history and culture.

It was only the institution of slavery as practiced by Europeans that sought to put blacks outside the circle of humanity. And for a few hundred years in the United States, they convinced themselves they succeeded. But history and human experience tell us different.

What we all know is that in exploring the particular, we touch on the universal. Whether it's Nia Vardalos's *My Big Fat Greek Wedding,* or a film by Akira Kurosawa about samurai in ancient Japan, or a short story by Isaac Bashevis Singer set in an Orthodox Jewish community in Poland, we relate to it because those stories are expressions of our humanity.

Take some of the most popular TV comedies of the last decades: *Seinfeld* took place in New York, *Cheers* in Boston, *Everybody Loves Raymond* on Long Island. Does anyone refer to these as "white shows"? Their casts and most, if not all, of the actors were white. And these comedies took place in cities where many African Americans live.

I believe that when Keenen Ivory Wayans created a hip-hop sketch comedy show, he was not making a black show, or a show for white people. He knew he was making something that the world had never seen, but that spoke to the human family.

Our performing cast included a gaggle of Wayanses (Keenen, Damon, Kim, Shawn, Marlon) and, among others, Jim Carrey, T'Keyah Crystal Keymáh, Kelly Coffield Park, Steve Park, Kim Coles, Jamie Foxx, Chris Rock, and Alexandra Wentworth. Carrie Ann Inaba and Jennifer Lopez were there as dancers and Rosie Perez as choreographer. The point was that they were the same as Keenen or me: We were part of *In Living Color* and we were living a life that wasn't black or white—just talented and funny.

Chapter 1

White Woman to the Rescue

My story is my own and it's unique, but it's also part of a larger story of my times, very much influenced by social and political currents and events. No one who went through those times came out unchanged.

I was born in Greenville, Mississippi. The woman who gave birth to me, Tommie Gene Reed, was an African-American single mother. When I was an infant, she could not care for herself, much less me. When I was around two years old, she abandoned me. She left me in a pile of garbage. That's the truth.

I know this because my mother, Barbara Jean Davidson, who is white, saw my foot sticking out from behind a tire in that pile of garbage and she rescued me. She took me to the hospital, and then decided to adopt me into her family. On the surface, that's dramatic, somewhat tragic, and redemptive.

However, there's more to the story.

When it comes to my family history, I have two different family histories. The first is a family I never knew. Growing up, I did not know my birth mother, nor, having been abandoned by her, did I seek her out. I had no idea if she was even alive, until I was nearly thirty-three. I was in New York, on the set of *Woo,* a film I was starring in with Jada Pinkett Smith, when my mom, of all people, called to say she had found my birth mother. This happened without my ever asking her to do so, or even wanting her to do it.

When I did finally meet my birth mother, Tommie Gene, face-to-face, I learned much from her that I am proud to know and that I would have never known otherwise, including that she was part Choctaw Indian and that my biological father was black and also had Native American ancestry.

My biological family, I learned, was made up of blacks and Native Americans, ex-slaves who were in Mississippi. Many of them took part in the great northern migration and settled, eventually, in Milwaukee. But learning that would come later.

When my birth mother abandoned me, she was at her lowest point. She was 100 percent defeated by her addictions, behaviors, and by her circumstances. You don't have to be a religious person or believe in a higher power to understand that there was some kind of powerful intervention that made it so my birth mom, who couldn't take care of me, abandoned me in a way that my mom could find me, adopt me, and raise me. There is redemption in that.

Now, as to why my mom, Barbara Jean Davidson, was in Greenville, Mississippi, when she found me. . . .

My parents, Larry and Barbara, were teachers living in Fort Collins, Colorado, when they listened to President John F. Kennedy's televised speech, "Report to the American People on Civil Rights," on June 11, 1963.

It is worth quoting that speech, in part, because the words ring as true today as they did when JFK said:

> One hundred years of delay have passed since President Lincoln freed the slaves, yet their heirs, their grandsons, are not fully free. They are not yet freed from the bonds of injustice. They are not yet freed from social and economic oppression. And this Nation, for all its hopes and all its boasts, will not be fully free until all its citizens are free.
>
> We preach freedom around the world, and we mean it, and we cherish our freedom here at home, but are we to say to the world, and much more importantly, to each other that this is the land of the free except for the Negroes; that we have no second-class citizens except Negroes; that we have no class or caste system, no ghettoes, no master race except with respect to Negroes?
>
> Now the time has come for this Nation to fulfill its promise. The events in Birmingham and elsewhere have so increased the cries for equality that no city or State or legislative body can prudently choose to ignore them.
>
> The fires of frustration and discord are burning in every city, North and South, where legal remedies are not at hand. Redress is sought in the streets, in demonstrations, parades, and protests which create tensions and threaten violence and threaten lives.
>
> We face, therefore, a moral crisis as a country and as a people. It cannot be met by repressive police action. It cannot be left to increased demon-

strations in the streets. It cannot be quieted by token moves or talk. It is time to act in the Congress, in your State and local legislative body and, above all, in all of our daily lives.

It is not enough to pin the blame on others, to say this is a problem of one section of the country or another, or deplore the fact that we face. A great change is at hand, and our task, our obligation, is to make that revolution, that change, peaceful and constructive for all.

Those who do nothing are inviting shame as well as violence. Those who act boldly are recognizing right as well as reality. . . .

But legislation, I repeat, cannot solve this problem alone. It must be solved in the homes of every American in every community across our country.

In this respect I want to pay tribute to those citizens North and South who have been working in their communities to make life better for all. They are acting not out of a sense of legal duty but out of a sense of human decency.

Like our soldiers and sailors in all parts of the world they are meeting freedom's challenge on the firing line, and I salute them for their honor and their courage. . . .

That speech inspired my parents, so they became part of the volunteers who went to the South to Greenville, Mississippi, to register African-American voters and immunize children. While they were down there, they met my birth mother and got to know her.

When they came back to Greenville a couple years later, they wanted to follow up and see my biological mother.

But she was gone. They heard that she left her youngest, a child, at a house where she had been living.

Being the curious person she is, my mom went to that address hoping to find out more about my birth mother and where she'd gone. She arrived at a raggedy old house that was full of people doing drugs. No one knew anything about my birth mom, nor did anyone say anything about a child.

As she was leaving, she noticed a pile of trash at the side of the house. Something made her look at that pile. And when she did, she saw a tire, and behind it a baby foot was sticking out. And that foot was mine.

She uncovered the trash. There I was, starved, and abused physically. There were bruises on my skull and a dent on the side of my head. Barely two years old, I had been left for dead, and I was already half-dead. But my mom took me into her arms and rushed me to a hospital, where I spent a couple weeks healing. By the time I returned to health, she had decided to adopt me.

My mom actually had to go through hell and high water to sign papers petitioning for custody, so that if the biological parent doesn't show up, she can take the child with her. So my mom did it all legally. She had temporary custody of me, and then after a certain amount of time, with adequate attempts to contact the biological parents and no protest from them, she could file for a legal adoption. When that day came to take me, she took me back to Fort Collins, Colorado, where I was raised.

My birth mom's name is Tommie Gene, so I was renamed Tommy. Originally I was named Anthony Reed by my birth mother, but my adoptive mom did not know that when she arranged for my birth certificate to be transferred to her family. She named me Tommy. Tommy Davidson.

* * *

My mom Barbara's family has an interesting history. Her dad, Gerald G. M. Spence, "Grandpa," as we called him, was a cowboy from Wyoming. Grandpa was a chemist and worked for the coal companies. He spent a significant amount of his career in Bolivia, where my mother spent much of her childhood.

Barbara's older brother is the famous trial attorney Gerry Spence, who was the attorney in the Karen Silkwood case and in many, many other cases. (Wikipedia says he never lost a criminal case as a prosecutor or defense attorney, and hasn't lost a civil case since 1969.) Her younger brother, Tom, was an artist and a political activist who lived for many years in New York City, and now has his own diner in Buffalo, Wyoming. The family has a big ranch in Laramie, Wyoming, which we visited often when I was a child.

Grandpa Spence was really a significant person in my life. One of the first things that I remember was when I was just four years old and playing "cowboys and Indians," and my grandfather told me, "I want to make sure that you're the Indians, because the Indians are the good guys." He said, "Tommy"—very distinctly—"I want you to know this. There were white people that didn't kill the Indians, and that was our family." He instilled that in me real early.

I was like the spoiled brat of the family. He took me fishing and gave me my first camera. He and his wife, May, spent their twilight years in Gold Hill, Oregon, and Medford, Oregon, where I spent a lot of time during holidays and vacations.

I'd go there every Thanksgiving. We would watch the football games. And he had a contest with me to name what country the players' families were from. I learned that, if it ended with "ski" that was Polish. "Brown" and "Wilson," those were Irish or Anglo-Saxon. I could tell you if a last name was Greek, German, Armenian, Italian, or Russian. I learned a lot about where the names came from. He was a believer in equality, and a believer in people, and he instilled that in me real early.

He'd take me fishing by himself in lakes in Oregon. We'd stay there all day, just talking about the world. He was getting me ready for a world of discrimination and challenges that I didn't yet know existed.

I didn't know my father Larry's parents too well. But I did spend a lot of time in Colorado with his parents and my cousins there. They were basically homesteaders and were among the first settlers of what became Colorado.

At family events, even as a child, I was the entertainer. I sang since I was a little kid. There was no church. It wasn't a spiritual family. My father was part of the counterculture. He was of a post–World War II generation that rejected their parents' conformity and their values. He was questioning everything. He rejected traditional religion. He rejected capitalism. Society was changing and he wanted to be part of that. Our home was a kind of hip, atheist, and agnostic family.

In 1968, when I was around five, my parents got divorced. Fort Collins was becoming more and more of a hippie town and my father joined a commune. That did not interest my mother.

She considered moving to Oregon or Wyoming, where we had spent time, but decided that she could best find work and continue to fight for social justice in Washington, D.C.

She was right, in the long run. At first, she was a secretary, but then she landed a job at Housing and Urban Development (HUD). She eventually became the union leader there for years.

In the short run, and as far as my life was concerned, her timing was not great. We moved to Washington, D.C., the week Martin Luther King Jr. got shot. We moved into what was then one of the worst black cities. There was a riot going on with tear gas, tanks, and federal troops. My sister, my brother, and I were lying on the floor in the car, wondering what the hell was going on.

Here's the other thing: Until we arrived in D.C., I didn't know I was black. I thought of myself as brown, like a brown Crayola crayon, and my sister, my mother, and my brother as peach crayons. When a cat has a litter, some of its kittens can be white and some black; it's the same for horses and dogs. I just assumed it was the same for humans, and that I was just the brown one of the litter.

When I found that wasn't true for humans, it just broke my heart.

We went to a swimming pool, me and my brother and my sister. My sister looks like Cindy Brady. My brother looked like David Cassidy. And all the black kids kicked our ass all the way home. My ass, too, because I was called a "white-cracker lover." When I got home, I went to my mom, saying, "I don't understand what just happened, because all those kids kicked my ass and were calling me 'white-cracker lover,' and I don't like white crackers. I like graham crackers."

Grown white men would chase me home from school. I barely made it in the door. My mom used to have us on the floor picking peas with the lights out. I didn't know then, but she had us ducking. This was too rough for us.

We moved to Wheaton, Maryland, an all-white suburb of D.C. It was also where I first heard the word "nigger," and I heard it all the time. I heard people calling my family "nigger lovers" all the time. It happened so much, I finally came to my mom and I was like, "Mom, who are these 'niggers'?" They seemed to be pretty bad people. We need to stay away from them. What's going on?

She said, "That's what people our color, when they don't like people your color, call them." Again, my head just split in half. The whole world was changed for me at five. I'm like, *What is this world we're living in?*

That shock doesn't go away. Telling you about it, almost fifty years later, I still feel its sting, how it burned into my soul and turned my whole world upside down.

Still, the love I felt at home from my mother and my siblings had no color. My mom was a very involved, very nurturing mom, very "I love you," very touchy. We would watch movies together. We were constantly touching each other, kissing each other, saying, "Love you. Love you." We always did things together. Their love was what would give me a strong enough sense of self to survive the challenges I have faced in life. But Wheaton wasn't for us either.

We moved to Silver Spring, Maryland, to an integrated housing development called Rosemary Hills which, to me, was paradise.

Our little housing development had a little backyard where I played with other kids, who came from all over the world. There, I was just a good kid from Colorado. Nuncie and Tuery were Vietnamese; Kwaku and Anana were from Africa; Nigel and Ricky were from Africa as well; Melander was from India; Lucy and Linda were from Guatemala; Mark Vitek was Italian; Graham was American. And we were all one. Just kids.

Our local school, the Rosemary Hills Elementary School, had its own song. We'd sing, "We're a rainbow made of children. We're an army standing strong." I believe they had borrowed one of the songs from the movie *Billy Jack* and changed the words. (The original lyrics are "We're a rainbow made of children. We're an army singing a song.") We used to sing it every day, and all the neighborhood kids were my classmates. At some point in the 1970s, Rosemary Hills was deemed "too black," and kids would be bused to other schools in the surrounding Maryland suburbs. (It's worth noting that they didn't decide to bus white kids to Rosemary Hills, just black kids out.)

That backyard was my cocoon. In the backyard, there was a square and in it was a raised platform, with logs surrounding it. That was my first stage.

Some of the women would point their stereo speakers out of the window and I would perform for the kids to the music. I would sing to the music. Or I would deliver my Academy Award acceptance speech. That was where I got my start—where my skills as an entertainer began. And I've always believed that the good Lord must have been looking out for me, because he put that little stage there for me to find my talent.

The music started coming on and I just came alive, and everybody got a kick out of it. They were like, "Look at this little dude. Look at him." What they would do was, they would all gather, get beers, and say, "Barbara, go get your son." She'd bring me downstairs, they'd take a spoon, put tin foil over it, lift me up on the table, and put on, "Say It Loud—I'm Black and I'm Proud." And I'd perform. I'd sing along, saying, "Say it loud. I'm black and I'm proud. . . . We can do the boogaloo. Say it loud. I'm black and I'm proud." I'd do this whole dance. It was Aretha Franklin's "Respect": "*R-E-S-P-E-C-T,* find out what it means to me." Sam & Dave's "Soul Man." I'm guessing there was a not-so-subtle message in these songs that my mom wanted me to learn.

I knew all the dances: the pony, the monkey, the jerk. I learned them all fast. Those were my first performances.

Because my mother worked, we were latchkey kids. Most days, the TV was my babysitter. I watched everything from Laurel and Hardy to *Gilligan's Island, Green Acres, The Andy Griffith Show, The Brady Bunch, The*

Odd Couple, Laugh-In, and *Love, American Style.* I was a huge Carol Burnett fan, a huge Shields and Yarnell fan, huge Sonny and Cher fan, huge Donny and Marie fan. I became a student of TV comedy—that, too, was part of my training to become an entertainer.

My mother encouraged my talent. Because I was always singing, at every opportunity, I started out doing talent shows when I was seven. These would take place at school auditoriums and community centers. I would watch a lot of other kids sing and dance, and I would then perform. My mom made this little jumpsuit that I would perform in. She would buy these pattern kits and then say to me, "Pick one"; then she'd sew it for me. I won everything in the metropolitan area as a singer.

My mom also took me to a lot of plays. Some of the musicals and musical movies I saw and loved were *Godspell, Tommy, Jesus Christ Superstar, Hair, Chitty Chitty Bang Bang, Bye Bye Birdie,* and *Cabaret.* My mom would say of a play we were going to, "You need to see this!" Afterward, when she bought me the cast album to play at home, she would say, "You need to learn these songs." She just knew.

My mom's best friend, my aunt Rosie, who was African-American, took me to a Jackson 5 concert when I was eight. After that, I learned all the Jackson 5 songs and all the Motown songs. I wanted to be the best singer in the world.

Everybody liked me because I could sing, and because I could entertain. And everybody loved my mom. She was like a community person. If something happened in the community, they turned to Ms. Davidson. Everyone respected Ms. Davidson.

A couple of days later, I was playing around on the railroad tracks, and some white teenagers spotted me. I knew the drill: I better run away, right away. It's "nigger this, nigger that."

"We can't wait to catch you, boy. We're gonna kick your ass!"

That's when two big old black guys appeared from nowhere, and I ran behind them. The white guys ran the other way, and I've been black ever since. True story.

There was a line drawn and I chose black. I've been living in color ever since.

I've always been able to pick up on racism, even before I intellectually understood what it was. I remember going into restaurants as I got older, twelve years old. I'd go in a restaurant with my family, and I'd get the vibe of "You don't look like them." I understood I was different. But my mother educated me. She had me read *Bury My Heart at Wounded Knee* when I was eight. She had me read *Lena,* Lena Horne's memoir, when I was, like, ten. Then she had me read Malcolm X's autobiography when I was probably about twelve.

When she gave me the Malcolm X book, the first thing she said to me was: "Before you read this, I want you to know that white people aren't the devil." I was like, "Mom, I know that." I knew that because my grandfather was a cowboy from Oregon and Wyoming, and my grandmother was this beauty from Texas. If you look at old pictures of them, she looked like Marilyn Monroe.

I had a friend in New York and, on occasion, my mother would put me on a Greyhound bus to visit him or my aunt Rosie. The bus would make stops along the way. I learned not to get off the bus in Baltimore. To me, Baltimore was the most racist city in the world. In Baltimore, if I was on the bus sitting by the window and a white man saw me, he would start yelling at me and cursing me. Sometimes white men would run after the bus. What they intended, I can't say. After a while, strangely enough, I came to enjoy what

I thought of as this magic carpet ride that whisked me away from the white men chasing the bus.

Our mom was always fighting the good fight. My mother marched in every march and for every social-progressive cause for workers' rights, civil rights, women's rights, gay rights. I used to say that for me, women's liberation meant the kids do the dishes and clean the house.

Whatever the cause, she took us along. We would help make the signs and the flyers for hours on end. Then we would post the flyers or hold the signs as we marched. Sometimes it felt like we were holding picket signs every weekend—sometimes in D.C., but also in New York. That, too, was part of our education.

Funny story: When I was in the first grade, we had to place our hands over our hearts for the Pledge of Allegiance. But because my mom was so right on, I did what she had taught me, which was to raise my fist in the Black Power salute.

The teacher was like, "Tommy, that's not funny. What are you, a comedian? Go to the principal's office."

When I got there, the secretary said, "So, you're the comedian? Hold on."

They had called my mother. When she showed up, we went into the principal's office.

"Your son's quite the comedian," he said.

"Everyone's been saying that to me," I said.

"What's the problem?" my mother asked.

The principal told her that I had raised the Black Power salute when the kids were doing the Pledge of Allegiance.

My mother nearly ripped his head off. "Are we in America? Is this a public school? Let me tell you, my son raised his fist because that's all the fuck he knows. We live in Washington, D.C." She didn't apologize. She just took me home.

I don't know what that principal was expecting. Maybe he was thrown off his game by seeing a white woman show up. Even so, I'm guessing he was not used to any parent, and no mother—certainly, no white mother—speaking to him that way.

Truth is, my mom was fierce. She was gangsta in defense of her family.

When I got home, she told all her friends in the building about it. And they were on the floor laughing. They had tears in their eyes. The picture of a little black boy with his fist raised, and then his white mom tearing the principal a new one, was more than they could take. It killed.

But our lives were not all laughs. While my mom was studying for her graduate degree (she would write her dissertation on Rosemary Hills and urban planning), we had to go on welfare. We were happy to have government cheese. So, when people say that people on welfare are just lazy or are cheating the system, I can tell you that my mother was trying hard to improve her situation, so she could get a good job. Welfare allowed her to do exactly that.

Another part of my childhood education (and not necessarily a good one) was my visits to my father in Fort Collins, Colorado. As I mentioned, he was living in a commune.

On the positive side, that was where I heard a lot of rock music, such as Iron Butterfly and Led Zeppelin. That was where I discovered Jimi Hendrix. On the other hand, I saw things no seven-year-old child should see: people having sex and taking drugs, all out in the open. They thought it was healthy to do so. They believed they were building a better society, creating a better world. However, even today, I can't unsee what I saw. Still, I got to spend time in Colorado, and when I was a kid, my life was pretty idyllic.

When I was ten, all that stopped. These real tough kids started moving in to the neighborhood. D.C. changed. Rosemary Hills changed. These were the years of the crack epidemic. Suddenly there was a lot more danger around us. I would get my ass whupped on the way to and from school. And people started cliquing up, because if you didn't have friends, you'd get beat up.

Where we were living now, in Silver Spring, there weren't gangs, per se, but there were groups. Groups of young black men. I fell in with a group. We all met when we were nine. In our group, the leader and chief troublemaker was Keith Mayo. And Tony Briscoe. These were the friends that I started to grow into. It was six of us. There're only three of us left alive, and one of us is incarcerated—that's another story! The rest are deceased. That was my crew.

By the time I was fourteen, like many inner-city black youths, we were lured down a dangerous path. My value system shifted. My ethics started changing: My sense of what it meant to be black was changing—or how a black teenager was supposed to behave and carry himself changed—I started hustlin'.

It began with shoplifting. I wasn't a natural thief. I was just trying to be like everyone else. More often than not, I was the guy who got caught. They would call in my mother.

She would show up. They would look at her. Then they would look at me. Then they would ask to see her ID to make sure she was actually my mom. Then she would take me home. And she was rough on me. But this was definitely a phase I was going through.

Our meeting place was this one black telephone pole, where we would hang out. I remember once we were standing there and Keith pulled out this gun to show me. I was interested, for sure. But it wasn't the first time I'd seen a gun. We'd also hang out in front of this liquor store and talk shit and throw dice.

There was a guy who we called "B", who lived in the apartments. He was much older and had his own apartment, but he would sometimes throw a football with us. One night, someone broke into his apartment and killed him. And there was another man, Ben, who was white, but was married to a black woman. He had two little girls and on Halloween he would wear a gorilla suit and chase us all night. He was a pharmacist and had just started working at a new pharmacy. It might have been his first day there, when someone walked in to rob the place and shot him in the chest. My sister and I witnessed a guy getting beat up with a crowbar in front of our house. A few years later, I saw my football coach get stabbed by his girlfriend in a hallway. And another time, I was in the lobby when I saw a guy get shot. So there was a lot of death around us at that time.

Keith and our crew progressed to selling weed. There would be guys you dealt with and those guys dealt with older guys, and so on and so forth. You gave them the money you collected, and they paid you. My mom would find stereo equipment in my room, or cameras under my bed, or extra money, and she knew I had no legit way to have that stuff. Once she was so angry, she threw me out of the house, and I went to live with Big Bill's family for several weeks in a building up the street.

I finally went back to our apartment and knocked on the door. She cracked the door open and said, "What do you want?" I said, "I want to come home." She said I could come home if I got a job. So I got on a bus and lied about my age and got a job at an IHOP in nearby Wheaton, Maryland, busing tables.

Our neighborhood became a drug neighborhood. You just had to stand in the street while the cars came by with people wanting to buy drugs. It seemed easy.

We thought we were tough. People would start fights with us. I remember once we were standing around, when a guy came up and said to Keith, "Hey, motherfucka, I heard you wanted to fight me."

Keith just looked at him coldly and said, "If I wanted to fight you, I wouldn't tell you."

That's some cold gangster shit. I never forgot that. He handled that moment in a way that shut down the other guy and ended the possibility of a fight. And he did it in very few words. Just a Sun Tzu *Art of War*–level warning.

Some of my friends started carrying guns. A gun cost fifty dollars. There was a guy in the building. You went to him, and for fifty dollars, he gave you a gun. They would do holdups of a crap game or poker game. But they wouldn't take me with them because they didn't want the word getting back to my mom. When the going was going to get rough, they'd always say, "You gotta stay home." But they let me sell weed and hang out.

We were into the music scene. Go-go, the uniquely D.C. proto–hip-hop music craze, had started. Even though I was just fourteen, we started going to clubs and seeing shows at the Panorama Room, the Masonic Temple, and the Howard Theatre. I had gone to summer camp in Rifton, New York, and made a friend, Willie Fields. He was the guy I used to visit in Manhattan by taking the Greyhound bus from Maryland to New York. Willie had introduced me to some of the first rap records ever made—and I brought them back to my school and my friends.

There were often shows at the local high schools, including the high schools in southeast Washington, which was the roughest part. We'd go over there just to see the bands, and then run all the way home. Or fight all the way home. That's when I considered myself to be a tough kid. However, we quieted down when my best friend got put in jail for stealing a car. I wasn't with him the night that it happened, thank God.

When I was in seventh grade, I threw a chair at a teacher. There was a rage in me and an anger that I didn't understand. I had a lot of problems in school. I was a smart student, but I just had a temper. I was considered a "problem student." When I walked to school with my sister and we were late arriving, she would be allowed to slip into class. Meanwhile, I was sent to the principal's office and then to detention.

When the principal called my mother in to see him, she didn't apologize. Instead, she asked him why her daughter, who was white, was allowed into her classroom, while her son, who was black, was given detention. And, not for the first time, I had to confront the ways in which my life was colored by race.

The principal wanted me thrown out of junior high school. Basically, he wanted me to sit out the rest of the year and then come back the next. He saw no way of changing the direction I was headed in, only a way to make his life easier.

Instead, my mother just took me out of school. For the rest of that school year, I went wherever she went. She took me to her work conferences, wherever they were, including one in Puerto Rico.

In Puerto Rico, we went to a roller rink, and somehow I started rapping on the sound system. They had never heard rap before. They liked it so much, they were willing to pay for a plane ticket for me to come back and do it again. But my mother said, "No, I'm not putting you on a plane to go be a rapper at a roller rink." And I was pissed. But my mother had other plans for me.

One time in Seattle, after the day's conference was over, all the attendees gathered at the edge of the Puget Sound. They built a bonfire. My mother turned to me and said, "Tommy, do some of the stuff that you do." I entertained the adults for the next couple of hours, doing my singing impressions and singing jingles from commercials.

That was a turning point for me. I realized that the good kid, the one who entertained his friends in the backyard, was still inside me. I didn't have to be the tough guy my neighborhood wanted me to be.

When we returned, I agreed to attend a behavioral school for two years, Mark Twain, which was embarrassing. I used to have to catch the little short bus in front of everybody. There were some students there with some really severe behavioral issues. But I worked through it.

Michael, my brother, who was my best friend, was a big help. He asked me why I chose to follow negative behavior.

"What do you mean?" I said, because I didn't know the difference between positive and negative behavior.

He said, "Well, 'positive' is when you build things, when you help people, when you're always doing something good. 'Negative' is when you're kicking over trash cans, and taking stuff from people, or robbing people, or selling drugs. That's negative." And it was the first time I really took a look at that.

After a year at Mark Twain, I went to another school, Sligo, for ninth grade. It was my first year without the kids I grew up with. It was like a clean slate. And I did really well, got B's and A's. I went to summer school and got my grades up so I could go back to high school with my friends that fall.

I couldn't wait to get back with my fellas. But when I returned, they were doing all of the same stuff and I had
changed. I started going out with a cheerleader. I would do
my homework. I didn't hang out with them anymore. And
they all dropped out that first year.

I was there by myself in school. And I did pretty well. But
I hadn't changed all my bad habits: I still drank a lot and
smoked weed like everybody else, but I just hung in there. I
started to sing again. The glee club, which was mostly
white, took an interest in me, and some of their members
told me, "We heard you got a great speaking voice." I
started doing the morning announcements at school and I
went on school trips with the glee club—that expanded
my horizons.

I had some great teachers. I had a history teacher who
loved me, and I always got A's from that teacher. I had a
science teacher, and I always got A's. I had a ceramics
teacher who noticed my work was good in ceramics. She
and my counselor, who followed us from junior high
through high school, tried to get me into Parsons. I used to
have my pottery on display at the high school, but I
wouldn't tell anybody. (I thought my friends would think
it was "sissy" shit.)

Through it all, my mother was one tough lady. We had
moved again, this time to Takoma Park, Maryland. However,
when she saw some of the shit I was getting back into with my
bad habits, she would just toss me out of the house. Told me
to stay with one of our neighbors in the building. Told me
that someone who was shoplifting or doing drugs couldn't
be in her house.

One time, after I'd been thrown out and a few days had
gone by, my mom passed me in front of a liquor store, where
I was hanging out. She just walked on by, like I wasn't even

there. It was cold. And it was the worst punishment I could receive—done without saying a word.

It made me want to come back home, so I decided I needed to get a job.

I started to work at Roy Rogers. I cleaned up there. There was a guy who worked in the back with me who was from Morocco. His English wasn't so good, so he would lean on me to explain things and tell him the right words to use.

We used to play the radio in the back. One of the songs they often played on the radio was Rick James's "Super Freak." He once asked me, "What's a 'super freak'?"

I tried to explain: "A freak is a girl who's . . . fine, looks good, and she likes to be with men." He didn't seem to get it. So I said: "You know how we have 'Employee of the Week'? Well, she is good at freaking. She is like 'Freak of the Week.'"

"'Of the Week'?" he said.

So I started to explain the lyrics to him: "She's not the kind of girl you would take home to your mother. . . ."

And he kept saying, "'Freak of the Week'?"

"Freak of the Week" became a running joke at the Roy Rogers.

Then after a few months there, I found out IHOP was paying a dollar more an hour, so I went over there. Having a job kept me off the streets.

Eventually I got a job at the cafeteria of the National Naval Medical Center. I would leave school after half a day and go to my job. It was part-time while I was in school and full-time when I was not. During the school year, I worked weekends and holidays there.

I still saw most of my old friends. They wore flashy clothes and had girlfriends that they showered with jewelry. This was all from the money they made selling drugs.

I can't say I didn't envy them. So with the money I made at the cafeteria, I bought myself clothes. Having my own money made me want my freedom. But I wanted more—beyond what I could afford.

When my mother found a camera, photo equipment, some clothes I'd shoplifted, as well as money she knew she didn't give me, and a gun under my bed (yes, I'd bought one for fifty dollars from the guy in the building for protection), she threatened to throw me out of the house if I didn't return it all and apologize to the people and places I had stolen from.

"There are three ways to make money in this world," my mother told me. "The first is to inherit it. Not a lot of blacks have inherited wealth. The second is to work for it, which is what the people did whose stuff you took. And the third is to steal it," she said. "The third way doesn't work for this household."

But the reasons I had the gun were serious. And there were things I had never told my mom. I never told her about the men who had abused me when I was a small kid. Or that at fourteen I fell off a roof. Or that a police officer stopped me in one of the housing-project hallways and put his gun barrel in my mouth. Another police officer had a vicious dog that he held in my face. Someone hit me with a cinder block and I got eighteen stitches in my head. I got stabbed through my hand. At one point, I severed my Achilles tendon. So there were reasons to be afraid and to want some protection.

And my mother . . . there were problems there as well. When she worked, she wasn't around, and when she was around, she had boyfriends who partied, and so I had some issues around that, too.

So my mother said if I wasn't going to change my ways, then I would have to leave. And being sixteen and thinking that I knew everything, I willingly left home.

I got an apartment with two older guys. This was my first apartment. And no sooner had I given them my rent and security deposit than they ripped me off. I had to wait another year until I was seventeen before I could move out again, but this time I got my own apartment in Hyattsville, Maryland.

To get my own apartment, I got two jobs. I got a job at a catering firm and at a home improvement center (like the Home Depot), which was perfect for my apartment. I had lost the cafeteria job at the medical center, however, because I wasn't in school anymore. (I then went to community college for a semester, though.)

That whole summer in my apartment alone, all I had there was all my high school papers, all my tests, and all my books. What I decided to do was put myself through high school again. I would have to be at work about four-thirty or five in the morning, get home at one in the afternoon, take a nap, and study all night. I don't really know, even today, what that was about.

That summer I read books. Read Malcolm X's book over again. Read a lot of my humanities books. Read a lot of Ibsen, Karl Marx, and some literary classics. However, one of the books that had the greatest influence on me at that time was *Your Erroneous Zones* by Dr. Wayne Dyer, which helped me form some kind of a psychological structure for my future.

"Make Your Vacation Your Vocation" was one of the chapters that stuck. When you work so hard on something, it has to be something you love and would do for leisure. This way, it's not work anymore. I started working toward that (and, really, that's what I'm doing now!).

I had a friend then, Jeff O. Dennis, and I'd met him when I was working in the naval hospital cafeteria. He was the first friend I had who taught me what friendship was all about. Before that, I thought of friends as accomplices—people whom you went with to steal stuff. Jeff was a friend who was there for me. He was like, "If you want to go to a movie, I'll go with you. If you're watching a movie at the house, I'll come over."

When I was living alone that summer, I was still smoking weed. I was still hustling, at least in the way I was thinking. When the lightbulbs stopped working in my apartment, I did what I used to do: I'd find a hallway in another building and take those lightbulbs.

Little did I know, I was headed for some revolutionary changes in my attitude and my life.

I went over to this other building, got in the elevator, and picked a floor at random. When the elevator stopped and I got out, I found myself staring at this big painting of Jesus. I looked at him and I felt like he was looking at me. Don't forget that I was high at the time. But that picture was looking at me. I paused for a minute. And then I thought, *Man, forget that, I got to steal.* So I went ahead and put lightbulbs into the bag that I had brought.

When I got back to my apartment, I saw something strange. The lights were all on. I was just standing there, thinking, *What the fuck?* I knew the lights were all dead when I left. Now they were all on. I thought something strange was happening.

Then my friend Jeff called me and said, "Can you see the light?"

I thought this was more Jesus talk, but then Jeff said, "I climbed in your window and your lights weren't working. So I bought you some lightbulbs and put them in for you. You can't be living in the dark, man. *Can you see the light?*"

I did. Both actually and metaphorically. That was the moment that I realized that I didn't have to steal anymore.

I had a friend and things could work out without resorting to stealing.

That summer was important in the redirection of my life. Taking charge of my reeducation was the start of a transformation of my life in terms of my values. My friends played a substantial role in that, in ways I could never have predicted.

At that time, I thought I was going to be a chef. I had my eyes on the prize. But life doesn't move in a straight line. When I told Howard Higdon, one of my best friends, that I had just scored a job at a hotel as an assistant chef, which is unheard of at nineteen, he did not congratulate me. Instead, he said, "You're a dumb ass. You are the dumbest motherfucker I ever met. You need to go do comedy."

"Where the hell am I going to do comedy?" I said. Turned out, Howard was working at the time as a bouncer at the Penthouse, a strip club in D.C. He had talked the manager into letting me go onstage.

Even by comedy club standards, the Penthouse was skanky. The worst strip club you could ever imagine. It's in the worst neighborhood, and the guards outside wore T-shirts whose backs read: *Please don't shoot him.*

Let me tell you a story about Howard and me. Howard was one of my friends since I was around eight years old. None of us was rich, but Howard's was the poorest family I knew. He had seven brothers and sisters. They ate in shifts. They had moving blankets on their beds. When we were kids, Howard came over to my house one Christmas with a paper bag. It had an orange in it and three plastic army soldiers. That was what he had received for Christmas.

My mother saw that and pulled me aside and said, "I want you to give him one of your watches." I did not want to give Howard one of my watches. I said, "Why?" And my mom said, "Because you have two. Your grandparents gave you one and I gave you one. You only need one. And Howard doesn't have any. And this will really make his Christmas special." So I gave him one of my watches, although I thought my mother was crazy for doing so.

Now ten years later, this is the same Howard who was about to change my life forever.

I told Howard I didn't know what to do onstage. Howard said, "I don't care what you do, just open your mouth."

I went onstage and started talking and doing some of my impressions. I told stories about the roaches in our apartment. I told stories about my sister and me. I imitated singers. I made fun of commercials. They laughed from the first thing I said, and I haven't stopped since.

When I decided to pursue stand-up full-time, my brother, Michael, was jumping up and down, because he kind of managed me during that little time. My mom and my sister were just scared. They're like, "What are you going to do out there? What are you going to do?"

In the end, my mother said, "As long as it makes you happy." She already had cried the day I told her I dropped out of college. She cried so hard. She said, "Ever since I found you behind that trash can, that was my dream. It was for you to get a degree." She said, "If I can make a difference in this little black boy's life, I'm going to feel like I did something."

After she passed away, I realized that saving me and raising me was my mom's greatest accomplishment. There's no doubt about it. Why would she move to Washington, D.C., if not to raise me in a multiracial environment? She was the one who encouraged my talent, took me to all the talent shows, took me to *Hair, Godspell,* and all the musicals. She gave me everything that fed my talent. And she knew that as well.

So she cried when I dropped out of college, but then she finally said, "I have to admit, me wanting you to graduate from college was an idea that I had. That was selfish of me, but it's what I wanted. As long as you do something that makes you happy, and you're not hurting anyone and you're able to make a living, then it's okay." I had her blessing and that meant the world to me. My world was about to change in ways I never imagined.

Chapter 2

Showtime at the Apollo

I was performing in D.C., first at the Penthouse and then at Ibex and Triples. I was doing comedy at places that weren't purely comedy clubs. That was good for me to get my feet. At first, you're just out there. You can't quite believe what you're doing there. It's exciting and exhilarating. It's frightening and scary. And it's a drug. It's a high.

I was doing comedy, performing for almost a year before I even went into a comedy club in D.C. Actually, I'd never been in one before, but I started going to open mics, at places like Garvin's. They had opened an Improv in D.C. around then, but I had not broken into that yet.

Once I took to the stage, I needed to educate myself about black entertainers, black performers, black audiences. In the clubs where I performed, I learned a lot from the older performers, many of whom still performed on the Chitlin' Circuit. They taught me to appreciate those that came before me, on whose shoulders I stood. I also learned a great deal from my audiences, black and white. I became expert in what would set each off in howls of laughter. From the clubs in Washington, D.C., to Harlem's

Apollo Theater, there was a whole world of entertainment history to embrace.

No one gets here alone. Coming up, I was greatly inspired by black entertainers who are part of the permanent culture of the United States.

Imagine American culture without black folk. You can't. There would be nothing to talk about. No blues, no jazz, no gospel, no rock 'n' roll. No Elvis Presley, no Bob Dylan. Internationally, the Rolling Stones and Eric Clapton would have had no songs to learn to launch their careers if there were no black performers. Take away Louis Armstrong, Robert Johnson, Sister Rosetta Tharpe, Chuck Berry, Miles Davis, Little Richard, Ray Charles, and what are you left with? Not a whole hell of a lot.

No one has danced the way the Nicholas Brothers did, nor the way Judith Jamison did. No one sang the way Billie Holiday, Sarah Vaughan, or Ella Fitzgerald did.

They are part of what makes American culture so great.

Black comedians have been making people laugh for so long, and so well, that white comedians used to put on blackface just to get a laugh. Moms Mabley exists in her own galaxy of talent. And Richard Pryor? There is comedy before and after Richard Pryor, and no comedy today without him.

The artist I most admire, Sammy Davis Jr., was the consummate entertainer. He could do it all—sing, dance, act—and he'd been doing it from the age of four when he started performing on the streets of Harlem. Sammy was all about love. He had a way of reaching the audience, regardless of his color or theirs, because he spoke to their humanity. And that's been a role model and a goal for me.

But back to my comedy career.

I was a success but a very local one. The Penthouse, the strip club where I first performed, remained my home base.

For a nineteen-year-old, going to work in a place full of naked women was reason enough to show up; hanging out in the dressing room with the dancers was an education in itself. I got good fast.

I was also appearing at the Improv in D.C., where I would perform for mostly white audiences. I didn't really have to change my act. After all, a white family had raised me, and they had been my first audience.

In these early days, I got to watch other young comics working out their material. One of the people that stood out even then was Dave Chappelle. Chappelle grew up in my neighborhood. He grew up on the "good side." He was kind of scared to be around us. He was nowhere even near a flicker of the comedian he is today. He was an unknown and real raw. But, like me, he was learning what worked and what didn't. That takes years. But that's how you build a career as a comic.

You know who was funny, even back then? Martin Lawrence. One of the reasons that we all went to Garvin's was that Sinbad performed there. Sinbad headlined on open mic night and that was big for me. That's where I first met Martin. He had a uniform that he always wore when he performed: It was this Adidas jacket and it was sort of like Eddie Murphy in *Raw*. And he was funny. When he wasn't performing, he was a quiet guy. Almost shy. But onstage, this loud personality came out.

For the most part, these weren't paid gigs. Once in a while, I would go in my friend Ron Suel's van with his friend Mike James to a military base in Virginia or a cabaret. But that was it . . . until I performed at the Carter Barron. That made all the difference and was the start of bigger things.

The Carter Barron Amphitheatre was a four-thousand-seat summer venue. It was run by Al Dale, who was legendary in D.C. for programming both the Fort Dupont theater and the Carter Barron for the National Park Service. It was said that Al Dale's summer community programs kept the peace on the streets of D.C.'s toughest neighborhoods.

Al had me open for concerts—musical acts. At the time, I was doing musical imitations in my act—which no one else was doing—so that set me apart and made me right to open for summer stage audiences. No comic in D.C. was doing big shows like that. So I took a big leap past a lot of local comics by performing in that big venue. I would do a twenty-minute set to get the audiences ready to hear some music.

I opened for Evelyn "Champagne" King, who had the hits "Shame," "Love Come Down," and "I'm in Love," and Starpoint (an African-American R&B group from Maryland, who later had a big hit with "Object of My Desire") as well as for Patti LaBelle and even Kenny G.

One night, when I was opening for Melba Moore, I was in the men's room after going onstage when a young singer in her band approached me saying he wanted to say hello and shake my hand. I had been used to meeting Patti LaBelle's fans, which often included a large contingent of gay church guys. So I wasn't sure about this fellow's agenda. I would have at least liked to have washed my hands, but I obliged him. We talked a bit. He was a great guy and he told me what a fan he was of my comedy. Soon after, he launched his own career, and that's how I also came to open for Freddie Jackson.

As for Kenny G, he really liked my comedy and invited me to do a few shows with him. At first, I wondered, *Why is this white-bread guy asking me to go on tour with him?* What I quickly found out is that Kenny is really hip. Kenny was a good friend of Kashif's, the multi-instrumentalist singer-songwriter and producer who had been part of B.T.

Express and had written Evelyn "Champagne" King's hit "I'm in Love." At one time, Kenny shared an apartment with Kashif. Kenny G and Patti LaBelle taught me a lot about show business. They showed me what being a professional meant and what it took to give a powerful and flawless performance.

I learned my work ethic from Kenny G, who would practice for an hour before every show, in addition to spending another hour for the sound check. That was a total of two hours of rehearsal before every show. Kenny did all that so his performance would seem effortless when he was onstage.

Patti LaBelle taught me something about performing. Patti would not only do an encore, she would always do two more songs. Every night. No one ever left a Patti show feeling cheated. I learned that from her.

As for comedy, I did have one mentor at the Ibex club in D.C. His name was "Catfish." I don't remember his last name—if I ever knew it. He was just Catfish, and he had performed in vaudeville on the Chitlin' Circuit, taking trains to St. Louis and Detroit. He had opened for a lot of jazz acts, and his own performances were like a bebop improvisation. He was a Moms Mabley kind of comic, always talking in a grumble of "motherfucker this, and motherfucker that," right down to the raw pork chop. Catfish could make me laugh more than any other comic.

Often he waited until after my act to pull me aside and give me advice. I remember one time he told me: "Listen to me, you little motherfucker, don't you ask nobody shit. Don't you tell 'em what you getting ready to do, and don't you ask them no questions about what you getting ready to do. You just fucking do it! Those motherfuckas came to see you. They paid a ticket and they come to see you, and they don't want no interview, no questions, they just want you to do it. When's the last time you went to McDonald's and told them how to make your burger? You ask for a Big Mac and they hand it to you. That's what you gotta do."

The Carter Barron also did something else for me. It gave me greater ambitions. Because after successfully performing at the Carter Barron, I decided I needed to do the Apollo.

The Apollo back then was some serious shit. It was not some clown coming out and making fun of the performers or the audience. It was the firing squad. You went out there, and you killed or were killed.

I started going up to New York to appear at the legendary Apollo Theater's Amateur Night. Today, everyone knows the Apollo Theater on 125th Street, between Adam Clayton Powell Jr. Boulevard and Frederick Douglass Boulevard, and Harlem is filled with million-dollar apartments and hip restaurants.

However, back then throughout the 1980s, Harlem was dying. New York was still suffering the effects of the crack epidemic. The main artery of Harlem, 125th Street, was a collection of discount stores and closed and going-out-of-business stores. There was no tourism, just street life. The Apollo Theater itself was being renovated in hopes of improving the neighborhood. Major concerts were rarely performed there, and its future was far from secure.

New York was not "fun city" back then, either.

I remember one time when I went up to New York. I had taken the Greyhound to Port Authority, which, in those days, smelled like a public toilet and was filled with predators looking for easy marks. I had to sprint from the bus out of the bus terminal to catch a city bus uptown.

It was winter, and it was subzero. There was snow everywhere. And you know that when it snows in New York, that means dirty slush and puddles as big as sinkholes everywhere. And I'm standing there in whatever outfit I'd put together to perform in, with whatever raggedy coat I was wearing, which didn't do much good.

I'm waiting on this motherfucking bus to come. And when I finally spot it in the distance, I'm jumping up and down. Not only for joy, but also to keep from freezing. And all I'm thinking is: *Man, I can't wait to get on that bus. . . .*

And then the bus pulls up, slows down in front of me, and this fat old white driver takes a look at me and . . . just keeps on driving.

And I'm watching the bus go off in the distance, and I'm cursing him and telling myself, "If I ever see him again, Imma gonna whip his ass!"

And then the same thing happens with the next bus.

But I was determined to get to the Apollo because it had tradition.

Who hadn't performed at the Apollo? All the greats had performed on its weathered stage: Louis Armstrong, Bill "Bojangles" Robinson, Bessie Smith, Duke Ellington, Dizzy Gillespie, and Count Basie. Same for Billie Holiday, Diana Ross and the Supremes, Sammy Davis Jr., James Brown and the Famous Flames, Jimi Hendrix, and Bob Marley. As for comics, Stepin Fetchit himself had graced the stage, as had Moms Mabley, Dewey "Pigmeat" Markham, and, more recently, Redd Foxx, Godfrey Cambridge, Bill Cosby, and Richard Pryor.

The tradition of the Amateur Night at the Apollo Theater still remained strong, as an inexpensive and fun way for African Americans to spend an evening among their own, shooting boos, applause, and encouragement to entertainers who might one day become famous. Among the entertainers who got their start at the amateur night were a seventeen-year-old Ella Fitzgerald and Jimi Hendrix, who won an amateur musician concert there in 1964.

When I took to the stage at the Apollo, I was still too

young and foolish to be afraid. I was just going to do what I knew I could do. It had worked for the crowds at the Carter Barron and I knew I could get over with the crowd at the Apollo.

Ralph Cooper, who had been master of ceremonies for fifty years, was there to introduce the contestants and to beckon us up those famous stairs that led from the dressing rooms to the stage. Cooper called them "the stairway to the stars," because the walls were filled with framed photographs of performers like Louis Jordan, Aretha Franklin, and Lloyd Price.

Back then, my act was talking about what city people knew: living with roaches, having to go to work, dealing with addicts and drunk people. I would become those characters, like "Larry the Drunk," who was always getting fired from jobs for stealing things he didn't even know he had taken. I knew guys like that. They justified their reality.

I had routines about black women and how they are psychic (they know all your bullshit before you say it), about the difference between the way white women and black women get angry, how older white guys get angry in short sentences ("You are out of line!"). Meanwhile, younger white guys get angry and stay friendly at the same time ("Dude, can I get you not to do that?").

I also did my imitations of singers such as Al Green, Lou Rawls, Anita Baker, Lionel Richie, Michael McDonald, Barry White, Peabo Bryson, Harold Melvin and the Blue Notes, the Chi-Lites, Blue Magic, the Delfonics, Michael Jackson, and Rick James. In fact, one of my bits that always killed was imagining singers like Rick James or Prince going in to order at McDonald's.

All told, I had about an hour's worth of material, and at each show, I would pick a different ten minutes of what-

ever I felt would work best for that performance. All
through the summer, I battled one performer after another,
until at summer's end I was in the finals.

I was good enough that the *New York Times* even took
note. In the article "Playing Again at the Apollo: Top Dog
Night," published on June 11, 1986, reporter Samuel G.
Freedman singled out that season's top performers, including "a comedian named Tommy Davidson who imitates
the funk star Rick James."

Despite my success all season and the press attention, I
lost to a singer, David Peaston, in the finals. However,
after my performance, a young black man dressed in a
conservative suit and tie approached me. He was named
Sinclair Jones.

Sinclair was a New York lawyer who loved entertainment and entertainers more than law. "One night in
1987," Sinclair recalled, "I saw a comedian perform at the
Apollo, and I said to myself, 'My God, this guy's incredible.'" Sinclair called it "the ten minutes that changed his
life." That comedian was me.

At the time, Sinclair was a lawyer at one of the big
sports firms in New York City, and he happened to be
there that night. He met me backstage and said, "Oh, my
God. I've never seen anything like you. You're incredible. I
think you can write your own ticket."

We talked, promised to stay in touch, and I headed back
home to D.C.

Sinclair came down to Washington, D.C., to see me perform my full set. Afterward, he sat down with me and said
that he believed that I could be one of the most successful
entertainers anywhere. He could see me doing not just
stand-up, but also TV and movies. But if that was all
Sinclair had to say, my life and his would have remained
the same.

Instead, Sinclair made me an offer, saying: "I'm willing to put my money where my mouth is. I'll take you to L.A. for a week, all expenses paid, with a place to stay. You perform at the clubs out there—and if you like it and it goes well, would you move out there and let me manage your career?"

Sinclair was willing to invest in me. That made all the difference.

I didn't think for more than a second. I said, "Sure," and soon enough we were planning our week in L.A.

I'd never been to California before.

Chapter 3

Stand-Up Is Easy, Improv Is Hard

My first impression of California? Truthfully, I wasn't impressed, because the whole way from the airport I had seen very little natural beauty—just freeways. We were staying in West Covina, a suburban community east of Los Angeles, past the tangle of highway interchanges in Downtown L.A. I remember, as we were driving on the 101 Freeway, seeing the Hollywood sign and we kept going. I kept thinking, *If this is L.A., it's not what I thought.*

Once we were in West Covina, the street life, the community's ethnic mix, was different than what I expected. I'm sensitive to the ethnic makeup of a neighborhood and I was surprised that where we were staying there were a lot of Filipinos, Mexicans, Koreans, and Chinese immigrants. Blond surfer dudes and beach Barbies—not so much. I thought it was weird, and much different than New York City or D.C.

That said, we weren't out there to be tourists. Sinclair and I were all business. That night, we plotted out our strategy for the clubs. You have to understand that in the late 1980s, there was no YouTube, no Internet. The only way to get noticed was to be seen—in person—live in a comedy club. Comics hoped to have some scout discover them and then to get a slot on a late-night talk show, like *The Tonight Show*, or an audition for *Saturday Night Live* (which rarely had black performers, and even then rarely more than one at a time). Then, if you were one of the lucky comics, you might get a role on a sitcom. A very few, like Eddie Murphy, got to do movies.

At that time, there were three comedy clubs in L.A. where we wanted to make an impression. At the top of the food chain was the Comedy Store on Sunset Boulevard in West Hollywood.

The Comedy Store was launched in April 1972 by comedians Sammy Shore and Rudy Deluca. The site was where Ciro's nightclub had once stood, and it eventually became a rock 'n' roll venue, too. In 1973, as a result of Sammy Shore's divorce, the club went to his wife, Mitzi Shore, who bought the building in 1976. She renovated and created a "main room," which could hold 450 patrons, and the smaller room, which held at most ninety-nine people. It was the dream of every comic to play the Main Room one day.

The Laugh Factory was second on our list. Jamie Masada had arrived in America at age four. By the time he was a teenager, he was hitting the comedy circuit, making people laugh in his combination of Hebrew, Farsi, and thick-accented English. He soon became friends with Jay Leno, David Letterman, Redd Foxx, and Richard Pryor. In 1979, when comedians went on strike against the Comedy Store to get paid for their performances, Masada opened the Laugh Factory in a building once owned by Groucho Marx. Richard Pryor was the first performer at the Laugh Factory.

Finally, third, but most important to Sinclair and to me, was the Comedy Act Theater. The Comedy Act Theater was the most important showcase for comedy for African Americans in the world. The Comedy Act Theater was opened in 1985 by Michael Williams in South Central Los Angeles. Williams recruited Robin Harris (who would go on to fame as the creator of *Bébé's Kids*) to be the club's emcee and talent coordinator. In no time, the Comedy Act Theater became the premier comedy club to cater to African-American audiences. By 1988, when I first arrived in L.A., Thursday was the big night there, when they mixed newcomers with stars. Jones called ahead and got me a Thursday spot.

That first week, I went to the Comedy Store on open mic night, picked my number out of a hat for the small room, did five minutes, and killed them. I went to The Laugh Factory on open mic night, picked a number out of a hat, and killed them.

Then it was Thursday, and I headed over to the Comedy Act Theater. They had two shows and I was going to perform in both. When we arrived, the place was crowded and getting more crowded. The air was electric. I saw so many famous faces that I thought that if a bomb exploded there that night, there would be no more black comedy. On that very first night, I saw and met everyone who mattered in "Black Entertainment": Eddie Murphy, Sinbad, Robert Townsend, Keenen Ivory Wayans, Damon Wayans, all of whom were doing stand-up then. Magic Johnson and members of the Lakers, as well as the Raiders, were in the audience.

And to show you how long ago it was: the Raiders were actually winning Super Bowls back then.

I didn't know enough to be afraid or nervous, I just went up there onstage and I destroyed the room: standing ovation! Second set: same as the first, a little bit louder, but no worse. The result was the same: standing ovation!

I'm a kid from Silver Spring, Maryland, meeting these legends. I didn't really even know who all of them were, but I was blown away. They were more than showbiz. They were in the entertainment industry. They had been working it for years. I was still just a guy who fell into comedy. For me, it was a high.

However, Sinclair was always a man with a plan. And that week, we made an important decision. There was no turning back. We were moving to L.A. Sinclair was very organized. He had a very linear ten-year plan for me to achieve success in comedy, then on TV, and finally on film.

I returned to D.C., and Sinclair to New York. I called Sinclair and told him, "I want you to manage me." Our plan was to save our money, every penny of our work money, to bank what we would need to pay for an apartment and as living expenses for ninety days. We figured that was how long it would take to make it in Hollywood.

Back in Maryland, I told Jeff (the friend who put the lightbulbs in my house) that I was going to move to California. I'll never forget this: He's sitting there. He's just a calm guy, you know? He doesn't bat an eye. I said, "You know, I'm going to move to L.A. I'm thinking I want to get into TV, movies, stuff like that."

Without even looking at me, he said, "Nigga, if I was you, I would've been long gone."

I said: "What do you mean?"

He said, "I've never really been around anybody who's as talented as you. I never told you that. I've never seen anything like you. For you to stay here, I was wondering what the fuck you're going to do with that, anyway? Why would you stay here?"

That was Jeff. He was killed on Christmas Eve, right before I moved. There was a lot of tragedy around me then.

My childhood friend Keith, the leader of my childhood crew, was murdered right when I got to L.A. So it was just like, good that I got out when I did.

It took six months, but the day came when I sold all my stuff. We packed up Sinclair's Nissan Sentra with my plastic Glad bags full of clothes and a big-ass TV in the backseat and headed cross-country.

We took the 295 down to Florida. Then we took the 10 all the way across the country. We drove all day, slept at night through Alabama and Mississippi to Texas, and across Texas into New Mexico, Arizona, and finally California. After a seven-day drive, we arrived in L.A., where we got an apartment in Burbank, California.

We arrived not knowing a single soul, except for my aunt Rosie, who now lived in Toluca Lake in the Valley. When I was a kid, she was the one who would take me to see the Jackson 5. She had moved to California because she married Robert Hooks, an actor who founded the Negro Ensemble Company and starred on *N.Y.P.D.* and about one hundred other TV shows and movies. (Actor/director Kevin Hooks is his son.)

Both Sinclair and I had jobs waiting for us: I got a job delivering mail in Downtown L.A., and he got a job with an L.A. law firm.

California still didn't look like I thought it should. As I unpacked in Burbank, I now thought, *Can this really be Hollywood? It's a bunch of old white people.* But I loved my apartment, and I delivered mail in the day and we hit the comedy clubs every single night. It was barely a living, but it was a life.

At night, the order was: the Comedy Store, the Laugh Factory, the Ice House in Pasadena, and we would wait for Thursday night at the Comedy Act Theater. I was all business at the clubs: no hanging out after the show. Our motto was to get it done and leave. I didn't drink, and I didn't smoke, and I didn't do drugs.

Days when I wasn't working at a job, I'd be working on my material at the house. My mandate was to hit as many clubs as I could and go home. Sinclair taught me that discipline. We also did "stopwatch"—timing my material—and we worked on it like it was the Gospel. I'm a bad motherfucka for a reason. He worked my fuckin' ass so hard, I started to wonder, *Why am I doing this?*

Finally I found a good job as a counterman at a Solley's Deli in the Valley, which made me happy because it hooked me back into my cooking career. I was really good at it, and the owners, Abe and Solley, really embraced me. They were very supportive. They loved that I was doing comedy and that I was a hard worker. And I also finally got a home club, the L.A. Cabaret Comedy Club in Encino, not far from where I worked. Every weekend, I worked there as an emcee, and that was my life.

For three years, I took three buses a day to work; I stayed up all night doing comedy and got up the next morning at five-thirty. It was a tough and, at times, monotonous routine. But I was doing what needed to be done.

Even so, it was a tough process for me to pick my name out of a hat at the Comedy Store, week after week. I had been a star in the micro-universe of D.C. and I knew I could get in front of an audience and get standing ovations. Still, I did five minutes every Monday for three years and never got on the main stage in the club. It was a humbling experience. But I also learned a lot hanging out at the Comedy Store during those years.

The Comedy Store was like one of those haunted houses you see on *Scooby-Doo*: dark, with a lot of rooms all over the place, and all these characters walking around. You would see stars there: if not in person, then on the walls.

There was Tom Hanks from when he practiced doing stand-up comedy for his role in the movie *Punchline,* Michael Keaton, Whoopi Goldberg. You'd see pictures of Moms Mabley and all these performers you wanted to be counted among. There was a real competitive atmosphere there—a million and one comics all trying to kill. To me, it was like the X-Men's X-Mansion: full of superheroes and freaks.

I was white-hot, anyway—at least in my own mind. I was still doing musical impressions, which no one else was doing, but I was also doing artists no one had even imagined imitating. No one was doing Lionel Richie. No one was doing Rick James and Al Jarreau—and making it funny. No one was doing Prince.

As a matter of fact, a year ago when I was with Jim Carrey at his house, he said, "I got to tell you, man, when I first saw you at the Comedy Store, you scared the shit out of me." He told me that seeing me made him change his whole act. "I didn't go back into the Main Room for at least four months after I saw you," Jim said.

I asked, "Why didn't you ever tell me that?"

He answered, "What was I going to say?"

Among the comics I met back then, Charles Fleischer changed my life. Charlie was the first comedian that I came across that can make you see ideas. Fleischer, who is today best known as the voice of Roger Rabbit, was famous for the ways he could change his voice and contort his face to create not just characters, but also concepts. You would leave his show and want to read a book. He could get onstage and do a joke about conception, make you see the egg, the sperm, and then imagine conception taking place. He is the most incredible mimic and the most clever and cerebral of comics. I thought, *This guy is fifty times more descriptive than Richard Pryor! If I can add that talent to my arsenal, that would be a hell of a thing.*

So Charlie set the bar for me to take on a certain intellectual depth and we became best friends. Charlie was one of the people where I saw how that was built. I saw kind of a blueprint there. At that point, it was just about going to the gym and just keeping on. It was about persistence.

In a similar fashion, when I saw Jim Carrey perform at the Comedy Store, I was like: *Whoa, I still got a long way to go!* (No matter what Jim says about seeing me, Jim took his characters to places I never imagined going.) I remember one routine he had where he impersonated Jimmy Stewart on LSD. It was so out there! When you saw Jim perform, you wondered if he would ever make it back. But he did. He brought it home every time.

Jim was a crazy man onstage, but in person, there was a different, more sensitive, friendly, loving person, hungry for community. In later years, a darker, more contemplative side of Jim would come out, but back then I knew the lighter side of Jim Carrey.

We became friends and Jim encouraged me to start doing more facial expressions and start worrying less about how I looked. Because I came from D.C., there was an urban code among blacks to dress sharp as a crease: There's a way that you do things and it's straight up and down. I had that uniform attitude, but Jim helped me break that mold. It was no longer about being the cool guy onstage. I no longer needed to be like Eddie Murphy, and I certainly wasn't going to wear red leather pants! Instead, I let it all hang out. Jim taught me that anything was possible onstage. He was, and remains, a comic's comic.

At the Comedy Store, I learned that there was more to comedy than just doing impressions. There was more to me that wasn't being revealed. I didn't know how to express that yet, but I knew that I would only get there from being onstage, trying new material, learning as much from the audience as from what I was putting out there. I knew

I had a lot of learning to do. Part of me felt I could kick anyone's ass in comedy on any given night. But it wasn't about one night. It was about a career.

Robin Williams was a genius. What came out of his brain was incredible. But Richard Pryor was a master. Richard Pryor's comedy had it all: It was physical, and it was intelligent. It played on our everyday assumptions, but it was radical in its intellectual subtext. That was my ambition. That was where I wanted to go.

At the Comedy Store, I watched and learned from so many different styles. I saw Jerry Seinfeld before he had a TV show: Jerry had a persona; he had a point of view; he had an act that was his alone. Same with Roseanne Barr— you only had to see a few minutes of her onstage before you knew she was a TV show waiting to happen. I watched Rosie O'Donnell, Ellen DeGeneres, Ben Stiller, and Adam Sandler. Each was unique, and watching each made me a better entertainer. As difficult as that time was, I am grateful for what I learned from it.

The other person that I learned from—who inspired me as I was developing my act—was, strangely enough, Bruce Lee. I saw an old interview Bruce Lee did in 1968. Lee was asked how it was that he was such a great fighter. His answer was "I practice so hard and so frequently that my body began to move at the speed of a reflex." What Bruce Lee talked about was that a reflex is something natural. So he practiced so hard that in a fight what was unnatural to do—martial arts movements—became natural to him. He no longer thought about what move to make; he just did it instinctually. Bruce Lee said that he came to experience "an unnatural naturalness and a natural unnaturalness." I applied that lesson to my comedy.

My goal was to practice so hard that my comedy and my stage performances came naturally. If I could do that, then it would be my moment. I envisioned myself as the

Bruce Lee of comedy. Everybody knew karate, but I also knew kung fu.

In Black World, I was a new, upcoming star. But knowing Robert Townsend or meeting Magic Johnson made no difference to my financial situation. However, the buzz on me from those Thursday shows at the Comedy Act Theater eventually got loud enough that even Mitzi Shore had to listen.

There were several stages at the Comedy Store. At the Belly Room, which only held about eighty people, Mitzi would let me kill in there. Then there was the O.R., which stands for the Original Room, but which I called the operating room, which was just off the entrance. It's a very dark room that holds 150 to 200 people. Mitzi had started to let me slay in there. Sam Kinison was this young, really hot comedian who was playing in there a lot. He was on the fringe, but there was no one else like him.

And finally, the big time, what all of us comics were gunning for, was the Main Room, which held about four hundred people. You'd see Roseanne Barr, Seinfeld, Ben Stiller, Adam Sandler, Jim Carrey, and Finis Henderson. Louie Anderson used to close all the shows after Jim Carrey.

For three years straight, I had auditioned for the big room at Mitzi Shore's Comedy Store. I had thought Mitzi such a bitch because she passed on me, over and over. Then one day, out of the blue, Mitzi called me to offer a spot in the Main Room. Two shows a night on Friday and Saturday.

If that was all, I would have already thought I was in heaven. Then Mitzi dropped the bomb. I would be on the bill with Eddie Murphy and Richard Pryor. Mitzi had made me wait, but when she came through, boy, did she ever come through!

Mitzi was very smart about comedy. The way she booked shows on the weekends was that there were two main slots: the opener and the closer. For some people, going on first meant you were the star attraction and people could leave after you were done; others felt being the closer was better because people had to wait for you and that built anticipation, and no one followed you. In between, Mitzi booked new talent, sort of as a palate cleanser.

When I got to the Comedy Store that Friday, I discovered the program was: First show, Eddie Murphy goes on, then me, then Pryor. Second show, Pryor goes on, then me, then Eddie. Four shows. I was between the two killers of comedy: a chance for the audience to recover and get their breath back. But that was not how I saw it.

I was determined to kick their ass. This was some chance for me. This was a shot at the title. This was my moonshot. It was Cape Canaveral time. I was hungry. I was ready. I was too innocent to know better.

Eddie Murphy was in his prime. He'd done *Beverly Hills Cop;* he'd done *Trading Places.* He was the hottest thing; he was on fire. He'd been doing stand-up since he was fifteen. He had such confidence—and charisma—that the audience was with him from the moment he took the stage. Eddie had an anger. He'd be so angry, talking a blue streak, and then he'd just break himself up. He'd do voices, bits about Martin Luther King Jr. in a disco, about Michael Jackson, boxer Larry Holmes selling Campbell's Soup. Eddie was a big fan of Richard. He called him the "Genius of Comedy," and thought Pryor's *Live on the Sunset Strip* was the greatest filmed comedy performance ever. But that didn't mean he wasn't going to bring it. And he did. He stalked that stage like no one else would ever own it.

Richard Pryor was always hot. Even when he was

fucked up, he was incredible. Pryor would just bring his life onto the stage. There was one night at the Comedy Store (truth to tell, I don't remember if it was that first night or another night we were performing at the Comedy Store), but Pryor's wife was hanging out just outside the back door. She was out there smoking, when this woman showed up. Pryor's wife went ballistic, saying, "Bitch, I told you to stay away from Richard." Suddenly wigs and jewelry were flying and it was a takedown nastier than any on *Wide World of Wrestling*. Richard had to go out there and end it. He brought his wife back inside. Then he went onstage and brought it all onstage with him, telling the audience about the women fighting, working it right into his act. It was some amazing shit. No one could make life into art onstage like that, while making you laugh so hard you are crying, gasping for air, and falling out of your chair. That was Richard Pryor at the Comedy Store.

There were so many celebrities in the audience, it was incredible. Stevie Wonder was there, the Jackson 5 . . . you name it, they were there.

And here I was performing for them, appearing between the two hottest black comics in the world. That weekend, it felt like I set their shoes on fire!

My comedy had grown since the days at the Penthouse or the Apollo. I still did some musical imitations. I still did Al Jarreau or Michael Jackson, with all the hand gestures and crotch grabbing, singing about buying the Elephant Man's bones. Now, though, I'd set those characters as part of a scene, making observations and using different voices for the different characters.

Backstage, Pryor had his room and Murphy had his own dressing room. That's where all the chicks and celebrities were hanging out. They stuck me in a little cubby, with no door, where I reviewed my bits.

Sinclair was there in the audience, holding a pad and taking notes the whole time. After each performance, he would sit me down and go over the whole show with me. I was exhausted, having run the whole night on adrenaline. I would complain, "You're going to kill me, Sinclair." He'd respond, "If you're going to be the best, you've got to know your shit." That's just how it was with Sinclair and me. All business.

During those shows, Eddie was very nice to me. He would come by and talk to me, but I was so nervous I couldn't really get used to feeling comfortable around him. He was such a big star to me. It would take me almost a year of performing at the Comedy Store before I felt I could talk to Eddie.

On the other hand, Richard Pryor didn't say a word to me. Not a word. Not a word until the last night of the last time we performed on the same bill. He was off in a big green room with food and women and whatever, and I was in this closet, a hovel really. That night, Richard Pryor walked all the way down the hall to my little closet, where I was by myself, and looked me up and down like I was some kind of strange animal. He shook his head and said, "You'z a funny motherfucka!" And then walked away.

I thought, *Yes! I'm on my way.*

I was able to quit my job because of that gig. I got thirty-five dollars a show. I did three shows a weekend. That equaled the same thing I was getting paid at the deli, so I quit.

A year or so later, Mitzi made me one of the new young marquee comics, along with Chris Rock, Meme Ali, Tamayo Otsuki, Pauly Shore, and a group called Piper and Tupper (a 1970s send up). She dubbed us "The New Faces of the Comedy Club" and booked us into her clubs in La

Jolla and in Vegas at the Dunes. It was on a trip to La Jolla that Mitzi told me the reason why she made me wait so long. "Because," she said, "I make the best always wait a long time." So I forgave her.

I loved hanging out with Chris Rock. Eddie Murphy launched Chris in the comedy world with a cameo in *Beverly Hills Cop II*. Chris played a valet parker who makes a fuss about parking Eddie's cement truck at the Playboy Mansion. That was a good push for his career.

The thing that I noticed about Chris that made him stand out from all the other comics at the time was that he was a thinking person's comic. Like Lenny Bruce or George Carlin, it was his word choice that made you laugh. Comics like Robin Williams and Richard Pryor had that skill, but there was a physical comedy that they used in creating a character or telling a story. Chris didn't really create characters. He was more of a pure technician, messing with the classic timing of premise, setup, punch line. There's also something subliminal about the way Chris works his stand-up. Chris gets a rhythm going in his act, and once he's got you caught up in that, he could be reading the phone book and you'd be on the floor holding your sides from laughing so hard.

All of which is to say, we were buddies from day one. Me being from D.C., and him being from Brooklyn, New York, we just hit it off right away.

The other thing that's worth saying is that both Chris and I were mainstream comics. Our comedy appealed as much to white audiences as black. We were in the clubs at the same time as Seinfeld, Bill Maher, Paul Reiser, and Roseanne. Chris and I were younger, and blacker, and hotter, so it was me and him. We were together during all those times. I went on tour with him.

And we maintained that friendship. Chris used my audiences on the road to prepare for all of his comedy specials. What he'd do is he'd call me. He'd say, "Man, when are you in North Carolina?" You know? I would say on such-and-such date. He'd show up on Thursday, surprise the audience, work his stuff out on Friday and Saturday. Go home Sunday. He did that for years.

But back to those early years. By then, I had moved my high school sweetheart, Desiree, out to L.A. to be with me.

I had met Desiree when I was ten and had fallen for her instantly. I was in Maryland. One of my friends had moved to this really nice suburb. I went to meet him at this roller-skating rink, and I spotted Desiree there. I didn't talk to her. I didn't know her. But I fell for her.

We went to different schools, had different friends, but every so often there would be a sporting event between our schools and I would see her there. I was too shy to talk to her. I just pined for her. Sometimes I would just walk by her high school, hoping to see her.

Now, if there was a right side of the tracks, that's where she was. Her family was affluent and quite well-known. In every way, she was out of my league.

However, during that summer when I was nineteen and performing at the Carter Barron Amphitheatre, I saw her one night in the front row—with her father. And she was looking at me!

By then, people knew who she was. She was famous because she had won all these beauty contests in Maryland and D.C. She had been in the finals of Miss Teen All American.

After the show, her father brought her backstage. Her father turned to me and said, "I'd like you to meet my daughter." I felt like I was in a Tex Avery cartoon and that like the horny wolf character, my eyes were going to pop out of my head. I took it from there.

After a little while, I had her connect the dots about all the times we were in the same places, but didn't meet. "That was you?" she said. "I remember that."

We were off and on after that. When she moved out to live with me in L.A., she already had a daughter, Jessica, who was about six months old. We'd been living together for a year or so and Desiree was about to have our first-born, Jelani.

I was now supporting a family and was very motivated.

Once the heat was on me from being one of "The New Faces," agents started coming to see me work the Main Room of the Comedy Store. They were like sharks smelling blood in the water. They were circling.

Chris Zarpas was a Disney executive who was a fan. He introduced me to an agent at William Morris, Cary Woods. Cary was from New York (the Bronx, no less). He was a very warm, very smart guy (he'd gone to law school at USC).

Back then, the audience was filled with show business people: TV and movie executives, casting agents, variety show bookers, actors (I met Winona Ryder and Uma Thurman there), and agents. Yes, it's true: Agents came to the clubs regularly. They would call you up and say, "What's happening tonight? You performing anywhere?" They showed up. And they brought their fellow agents, as well as their new clients.

The agents then were involved in the "show" part of show business. To my mind, today they are way too focused on the "business" end of it and not involved enough in the "show" part. They see themselves as dealmakers, not talent promoters.

So I was lucky when I finally signed with Cary Woods at the William Morris Agency (as it was called then). Best thing that happened to my career. Cary had only a few clients: Matt Dillon, Andrew Dice Clay, Gilbert Gottfried, Winona Ryder, Uma Thurman, and now me. That was it. Cary started to work for me.

Things were happening for me. Robert Townsend remembered me. I was kicking ass so good that he put me on one of his *Robert Townsend and His Partners in Crime* specials. It was my first cable-TV appearance.

Then Arsenio put me on his show. That was my stand-up debut on network TV, and I was wearing the worst sweater you've ever seen.

Very soon after, Disney offered me a holding deal for something like $150,000 for two years. Warner Brothers offered me a role in a new sitcom they had ordered called *Murphy Brown.*

At the same time, I got offered a TV pilot from Eddie Murphy, who had a TV deal with Paramount to develop the TV version of *Coming to America.* I was to play the king's little brother, who is now coming to America.

Robert Townsend helped me make the decision. I called Robert and I said, "I'm really mixed up, man. I don't know what to do." He said, "Well, tell me what's going on." I told him and he said, "Well, Disney's out. If that's the last hundred and fifty thousand you think you're ever going to make for the rest of your career, sign that deal."

Robert then left it to me to decide between *Murphy Brown* and Eddie's deal. *Murphy Brown* on paper was cool. It was a good script, but I was just going to be one of the cast members supporting Candice Bergen. My other choice was to be the lead in *Coming to America,* which had been a monster movie hit. So to me, it was the obvious choice. What could go wrong?

A lot . . . I found out. Even though *Coming to America* was being produced by Eddie Murphy's company, Eddie didn't want anything to do with the pilot. That hurt me at the time. I thought that if the man's name was on it, he should care. But now I know, it was just the studio trying to milk their property. If it succeeded, Eddie would have been happy to cash their checks. If it didn't, it didn't touch him. It had nothing to do with his career.

The studio hired a veteran sitcom writer to write the show. He came from the golden age of comedy. You know, setup, joke, joke, joke. He had no feel for Eddie, no feel for black pride. He wasn't African-American, but that didn't matter. I would have chosen funny over black. Eddie never visited the set. Never dropped by to see the show being filmed. I was just over there at that stage at Paramount, working my ass off, trying to get this thing funny.

Paramount knew they had a turkey. They aired the pilot a year after we shot it, on the Fourth of July, no less. Who's going to watch that? It tanked. That was that. All that work was down the drain. All those other opportunities were gone. I had gone from red-hot to stone-cold. But I wasn't giving up yet. And neither was Sinclair or my agents at William Morris.

While we were waiting for the *Coming to America* pilot to air, I got an audition for a new show that was going to be a spin-off from *The Cosby Show*. It was called *A Different World*. The show was set at fictional Hillman College, a traditionally African-American college like Morehouse or Howard University. There was some irony in the fact that instead of going to college, I had come out to Hollywood, and here I was auditioning to play a college student.

I met with the producers and tested for the role. I brought everything I had to that audition. I'd been out of work for more than a year, so I was serious about nailing it. They liked what I did and had me wait outside.

Another actor, Kadeem Hardison, who had appeared once on *The Cosby Show* as one of Theo Huxtable's friends, went in. They must have liked what he did because they had Kadeem wait outside as well. They asked me in again and once again I gave it my all. They asked me to wait outside. Kadeem went back in. He came back outside. They asked me in again. I did my best. And then I went outside to wait again.

However, this time as they opened the door for Kadeem to come in, they all stood and started applauding. As he stepped in the room, they started to give him hugs. As you can probably guess, Kadeem got the role.

I took that loss hard. I wanted to pack my bags and head back to D.C. I had worked at the hospital and I knew I could make a good living as a cook. Back in D.C., I had an apartment and a car. It was a real life. I was now a grown-up man. I had kids. I didn't want to put myself at the mercy of so fickle a system.

I went home, dejected. As I was making my way to my apartment, I stopped to open the mailbox and get the mail. Inside was a note from my mom. There was a twenty-dollar bill inside, and she wrote, *First of all, I know you need it. Second, don't come home. Keep on truckin'.* I started to laugh. Suddenly my problems didn't seem so bad.

I went back to working at the deli; I continued to warm up audiences for other people's sitcoms. I even warmed up the audience for *A Different World,* which poured salt in the wound and took the sting away—all at the same time. But it was a gig and I did what I do, as well as I could. I continued to perform at the L.A. Comedy Club. It was a grind, but I've never been afraid of hard work. Really, if I look back on that time, I would say that my dreams had come crashing down, and I was just a working stiff.

Then one day, Michael Gruber, a TV agent who was part of my team at William Morris, called to tell me that Keenen Ivory Wayans had a pilot called *In Living Color.* And you know what? I said, "No."

I told Michael that I couldn't take any more TV letdowns. I was near broke, but at least I had a job at the deli. I was trying to make rent and take care of my wife and two kids and working the clubs again. So I turned it down.

Gruber knew a thing or two. He'd taken George Clooney from aging sitcom bit actor to megastar and had been instrumental in making the careers of Queen Latifah, Ice Cube, and Martin Lawrence. He just understood the business and when to pounce on an opportunity. What he said to me was, "What's the downside? You audition and either you get it or you don't. And if you do, you can pass, if you want to pass. But let me tell you, everybody's being asked to do this show. All your contemporaries, Jim Carrey, everybody who's anyone who's funny."

And when he put it that way, like I had nothing to lose, I said, "All right, I'll fucking do it."

The auditions were held at a Fox-owned lot on Sunset Boulevard in Hollywood, the KTTV Fox Television Center. I was directed to show up at an office on the lot. Keenen was there with his producer, Tamara Rawitt. I sat down on a couch.

I had been doing auditions for a while now. What I was used to was being given pages of a scene and asked to perform them. What I had never done was improv. If I'm being totally honest, I'm not sure I even knew what "doing improv" meant.

So, what happened was, I was sitting on the couch, waiting to be given my scene, when Tamara said, "Okay, now you're a Puerto Rican cabdriver and somebody set the seat on fire in the backseat."

I had no idea what to do with that. Same when they said, "Now a fat lady's in the elevator with you, and she just farted."

I was terrible. I tanked. And I left there thinking, *What the fuck?* It made me feel worse. But there must have been something about me that they liked because they told me that there's a stand-up audition I could do. Thirty comics were going over to the Laugh Factory to have a show-down. When I heard that, I thought, *Now you're talking my fucking language!*

You name 'em, they were there: D.L. Hughley, Martin Lawrence, Second City performers from Chicago, Margaret Cho, Susie Essman. It was wall-to-wall comics. I was number 30 on the list. Thirty out of thirty.

Sinclair goes, "I don't want you to watch the show, man. Just stay calm." We went out on Sunset Boulevard and Sinclair put me through my paces, going over what material I was going to use. We went over that shit for what seemed like two hours.

They finally came outside and said, "You're on, man."

I said, "All right."

Sinclair looked me in the eye and said, "Just do what you do, man."

It was packed; Keenen is a genius at creating energy and buzz around his projects. People just wanted to see the action.

I did some of my killer bits: My Spanish neighbors, some of my imitations of Michael Jackson and other singers. And then, suddenly, right there, I had an idea. *RoboCop* had been a big movie – Everyone knew it. And I got it into my head to do Mike Tyson as RoboCop, so I did it. It was so fresh, and so funny, and so dead on. I guess it showed I could do characters and scenes and, in that moment, I understood what improv was.

Everyone stood up and starting applauding. Which was my cue to leave the stage. Always leave 'em wanting more.

Sinclair and I went back outside. We were just grinning and laughing. Suddenly Keenen popped outside. He came over to me and said, "I can guarantee you one thing. Of everybody in there, you already got the show."

I was the fortunate one.

Chapter 4

Making a "Living"

Before the L.A. auditions, Keenen had held auditions in New York and in Chicago. He had auditioned future *SNL* cast members Rob Schneider, David Spade, and Adam Sandler. (Keenen passed on the first two. He wanted Sandler, but couldn't get him.) Chris Rock knew Keenen and fully expected to be a writer and performer, but never got an offer from Keenen. Kim Coles was spotted in New York and invited to audition in L.A. From Chicago, he had invited T'Keyah Crystal Keymáh and Kelly Coffield to audition in L.A. They made the cut. From the L.A. auditions, Keenen passed on Martin Lawrence, D.L. Hughley, Susie Essman, and Margaret Cho.

When we first assembled on Stage 7 at the Fox Television Center on Sunset Boulevard in Hollywood, I knew some of the other actors/comedians: David Alan Grier, Jim, and Damon. T.J. McGee was one of the stars of the Comedy Act Theater, famous for his impressions. Toney Riley was another comic I knew from the Comedy Act. Jeff Joseph was both a cast member and writer. Damon was hired as a writer, but would also be a featured cast member. This was the first time I met Kim Wayans, Kim Coles, Kelly, and T'Keyah.

We were there to meet with the writers and come up with sketches. We knew that we would shoot more than we would use for the pilot; the pilot would have only the best of what we did. It was collaborative and competitive, all at the same time.

I knew this was a huge chance for me. I had already been doing stand-up for more than six years, living in L.A. for more than three and my pilot had come and gone. Keenen and Damon Wayans, Jim Carrey—these guys were heroes to me. They had been in L.A. for more than a decade and had been in movies! They were stars.

Keenen brought in Tamara Rawitt to produce the show. Rawitt had worked for Paramount in their East Coast marketing department during Eddie Murphy's hot streak at Paramount with *48 Hours* and *Beverly Hills Cop*. Murphy had asked her to head up his production company at Paramount in L.A. After two years with Eddie's company, she took a job as an executive at United Artists.

While working for Murphy, Rawitt had met Keenen. As I heard it, Eddie and Keenen were riffing one time on blaxploitation movies. Eddie said they should make one and call it, *I'm Gonna Git You Sucka*. Somehow Rawitt heard about that (probably from Keenen) and loved the idea. Eddie gave it to Keenen at no cost, and, to Keenen's credit, he wrote one funny movie that United Artists agreed to finance at a low budget, with Keenen directing. Although it was an MGM/UA motion picture, Fox had the distribution rights. Keenen starred alongside Isaac Hayes, Jim Brown, David Alan Grier, Robin Harris, Chris Rock, and a full complement of Wayanses, including Kim, Marlon, Nadia, and Shawn.

I'm Gonna Git You Sucka had this sly way of making you feel like you were in on a joke—a joke against Hollywood, African-American stereotypes, and the culture generally. More important, it caught on. Made for around $3 million, the film reportedly made Fox more than $10 million in its release. And Fox banked a significant part of that coin. So they were big fans of Keenen.

Fox TV was trying to distinguish itself in the marketplace by being younger, cooler, and edgier—the bad boys of TV—compared to the other staid networks. They approached Keenen and Rawitt about doing a show. Keenen pitched his vision of a sketch show that would take on *Saturday Night Live,* and it would have hip-hop dancers performing between the sketches. Fox's own studio, Twentieth Television, passed. However, Chris Albrecht, who was a former stand-up comic and former manager of the Improv in New York, had landed a job at HBO to develop original programming and signed on to produce the pilot.

Albrecht suggested Keenen hire Kevin Bright, who had worked on a few HBO comedy specials, to be a producer on the show. For the pilot, Keenen, Rawitt, and Bright assembled a diverse group of writers. Rob Edwards was a young black writer who'd worked on *A Different World.* Buddy Sheffield had written for *Saturday Night Live,* where he was Eddie Murphy's favorite writer and had cowritten *Coming to America.* (The fact that he was a white guy from Mississippi only underlines that funny has no color.) Jeff Joseph was a black stand-up Keenen liked; Howard Kuperberg had worked on *The Smothers Brothers Comedy Hour,* a 1988 reboot of their legendary variety show and was totally old school; and Sanford "Sandy" Frank, a Harvard Law graduate, had written for *The David Letterman Show* and had gained a permanent spot in comedy legend as the author of one of Letterman's most famous bits, "the Velcro Suit."

Each day, the writing staff would come up with sketches, and then Keenen and Tamara would pick through them. Sometimes, cast members would bring things they did in their acts to the writers to see if they could use them. It was a very creative and collaborative process that yielded a great deal of material.

We would read the sketches. Some would survive, more would not. There would be talk of costumes and casting for each sketch. We would rehearse them. But we had no firm idea of what was in and what was out. The production people were trying to figure out their needs. It was chaotic. On the other hand, a lot of great material was being generated.

Keenen and Tamara's plan was to shoot the pilot twice, on two consecutive nights, with a different audience for each night. That way, they would have two takes of each sketch to work from when editing.

Keenen asked me to warm up the audience for the pilot because he knew my stand-up skills were strong.

That first night, I had so much nervous energy that while I was warming up the crowd, I banged my leg into a light or other piece of equipment. I didn't notice anything because the crowd was laughing and I was in the zone. But when I went back to the dressing room afterward, I saw that my sock was soaked with blood. I almost passed out.

So when you say, "Break a leg," I almost did, right there and then.

The original presentation pilot opened with Keenen appearing onstage to introduce the Fly Girls and the show's DJ, DJ Daddy Mack, who was wearing a top hat with an emblem on it in the shape of Africa. Here's some Black World trivia for you: Daddy Mack was, if I'm not mistaken, son of producer and actress Dolores Robinson and brother of Holly Robinson Peete.

Back to the pilot: Keenen then led the camera backstage to meet the cast and crew.

"I'll tell you what I'm most proud of. . . . Unlike other shows, I've got nothing but qualified black people backstage making decisions." Keenen opened the door to the writers' room and you see white writers running out. Keenen explained they're the cleaning staff, and then introduced the black cleaning lady as the head writer.

"Now I'm going to introduce you to our cast," Keenen continued as he mentioned each cast member's name, their last name is always Wayans: "Jim Wayans, Tommy Wayans, Toney Wayans." It was a joke, but like all good jokes, it had an element of truth in it.

Keenen talked about what a big happy family we were, and then opened a door marked WHITE CAST MEMBERS ONLY, where Jim and Kelly are shining shoes and ironing shirts and singing "Camptown Races," a well-known minstrel song. Keenen remarked, "Oh, those people. Always singing, always happy."

I will say that this type of race reversal, or poking fun at racial stereotypes—saying they are long gone, but showing they are still prevalent—was not just Keenen's sensibility. If I was a betting man, I would guess that was the work of either Buddy Sheffield or Sandy Frank. Both of them were very self-aware white writers who were all too cognizant of the gap between political correctness and reality. They delighted in skewering it.

Keenen then did a bit where he said he refused to be silenced, while the censors bleep out what he's saying (a very time-worn comedy gag). This led into the series of sketches that followed.

The pilot had this "meta" quality to it. Keenen was riffing on the making of a diverse sketch show, not only with the opening bits about the writers and cast, but with an ongoing joke. In this running gag, Kelly (one of two white cast members) played a viewer who was writing an angry letter to the network about the show.

Now, if you are a student of comedy, and have done the deep dive on black TV history, you might recognize this opening as being very similar to how Richard Pryor opened his own show. Richard was one of Keenen's heroes. So whether this was an homage, a tribute, or a borrowing, either subconscious or conscious, I can't say, but it would be cut before the show's actual airdate.

Now, that being said, Keenen learned a lot from Richard's example about doing a variety show. The most important thing he learned was talent potential. Keenen understood how to play talent forward, how to stack a backfield with talent. Keenen understood all that. He had Bill Belichick shit going on. That is one of the reasons *In Living Color* was as good and as fresh as it was.

As for the sketches, let me make one personal comment about the process of filming the sketches. Just as I was a novice at sketch comedy, I had very little experience in being on-camera.

Despite how bad I wanted this, when the time came for me to act in my first sketch for the pilot—and it was just me and the red light—I felt the pressure. There was pressure to live up to these stars, the pressure of how much was riding on this for me. This was the big chance I needed.

I froze. I couldn't say a word. I couldn't move. Tamara Rawitt ran out on the stage and said, "Are you okay?"

Then Tamara did something strange. She handed me an apple and said, "Eat the apple." So I bit the apple, and I started to relax.

Then Damon came up to me. He looked me straight in the eye and said: "You worked your ass off to get to this point, and everything you got you deserve. You got your kids to think about. You got this damn career to think about. And you're going to lose your mind now? No way. You gotta do what the fuck you gotta do. So, nigger, let's get it up out of you. Let's go." And then he added, "Plus you're good, no matter what you do."

That meant a lot to me coming from Damon.

Damon's responsible for getting me over that hurdle, and I will always be grateful because after that . . .

The red light went on, and I turned on.

There were many great sketches we shot that didn't make it into the pilot. There was a sketch that I loved that made fun of Chuck Woolery and *Love Connection,* only in our version the contestants were Robin Givens and Mike Tyson. That was held for later.

I had a sketch where Sammy Davis Jr. had decided to do a Broadway show where he starred as Nelson Mandela. I did my imitation of Sammy, in all his swagger, performing in *Mandela! The Musical.*

Some of the song parody lyrics were: "Whether I'm right, whether I'm wrong, no cat's gonna stop this ebony star from singing my song. I gotta be free."

Or, "Mister Steve Biko, Mister Steve Biko, march."

And: "Who can take an apartheid, turn it inside out? Show these Afrikaners what this freedom gig's about? The Mandy man can. The Mandy man can. But they threw me in the can and threw the key away."

It was some brilliant Sammy material. It was in the pilot that we made for Fox, but it never aired because after we shot the sketch, Davis announced that he was battling cancer. It no longer seemed appropriate to mock him (much as I argued that Sammy himself would have loved it).

One of the most controversial and polarizing figures at the time was Louis Farrakhan, the leader of the Nation of Islam. So, of course, Keenen had a sketch that was a take-off of *Star Trek: The Wrath of Khan* called "The Wrath of Farrakhan." Jim played Captain Kirk, and Damon played Farrakhan, who appeared on the starship *Enterprise* to take over the white power structure, which was oppressing the minorities on the spaceship.

It was funny. But it was also very Keenen. Most of America, and certainly all of white America, thought Farrakhan was a bad guy: a racist, anti-Semitic Holocaust-denying con man. For which there is evidence to be found. And which is why it worked to cast him as the villain, the Khan of the sketch. But Keenen took a certain pleasure in pointing out that certain aspects of Farrakhan's critique of the roles of African Americans in the white power structure were on target. It was a warning that you could never second-guess Keenen.

The more we worked together, the more convinced I was that the show was going to be successful.

When we filmed the pilot, the audiences went crazy, laughing their asses off. That felt good. And the second night was just as good as the first. Keenen was like the proud papa. We all felt good. We all knew that we had made something that no one had ever seen on TV and it was going to be an immediate smash sensation. It felt so right.

And then we waited. And waited. And waited.

In Living Color was enough of a departure in so many ways that Fox hesitated about going forward. Or as David Alan Grier once said, the pilot was fun, but it was so outrageous he never thought it would get on the air.

Barry Diller, then head of the Fox Network, was nervous about airing *In Living Color*. He was afraid that some wouldn't get the humor and was concerned that some viewers would think the show was making racist jokes.

"Barry Diller was terrified of the show," Tamara told *Details* magazine, and as it later appeared on the website MentalFloss, she said, "He showed it to the NAACP. The NAACP was comprised of older members of the black community, and this was a hip, sassy, tongue-in-cheek show, so I don't think they got a lot of the humor." Before airing it, the network wanted to bring in members of organizations like the Urban League as consultants, but Keenen refused.

The arguments for airing *In Living Color* were pretty evident. *Saturday Night Live* had been on the air for fifteen years. Its casts were overwhelmingly white and, at that moment in time, everyone thought *SNL* was on the way out. No one could imagine that it would still be on the air today, forty-five years after its 1975 debut. ABC had tried launching a rival program on Friday nights, *Fridays,* which failed (although it is notable for launching the careers of Larry David and Michael Richards).

Fox wanted to distinguish themselves in the marketplace. Steve Chao, the genius programmer behind *Cops,* had rebooted reality TV. A show about cops posing as teenagers, *21 Jump Street,* had launched the career of Johnny Depp. Tracey Ullman's sketch show had introduced *The Simpsons.* And speaking of dysfunctional families, Fox's top-rated sitcom was the trashy *Married With Children* (launching the careers of Ed O'Neill, Katey Sagal, and Christina Applegate).

However, no TV network had tapped hip-hop and the demographically desirable hip-hop audience of eighteen-to thirty-five-year-olds with disposable income. Keenen had made Fox a boatload of money with *I'm Gonna Git You Sucka. The Cosby Show* and its spin-off, *A Different*

World, were both top TV programs, and Eddie Murphy was the king of the box office. This was a cultural trend that *In Living Color* was poised to leverage. We knew this was the right time.

I knew *In Living Color* was pure entertainment, and I had complete confidence that once audiences saw it, the show would be a success. Still, I was taking no chances.

I went back to work at the deli and the clubs. I warmed up audiences for every show possible to make a living. Thirty dollars a gig here, twenty-five dollars there; I even did warm-up for *The Price Is Right.* The cast, writers, and producers of *In Living Color* all sat around for the next six months. Some cast members went back to stand-up or their careers.

However, while Fox hesitated, it began to seem like everyone in Hollywood had seen the pilot for *In Living Color.* Tapes were circulating from agency to agency, from producer to producer. It became the worst-kept secret in Hollywood.

Whenever I did stand-up, people would come up to me after the show to talk about the pilot for *In Living Color.* David Alan Grier had the same experience. My agent, his agency, David's agent, his agency—everyone had seen the pilot. It was insane.

Then something happened that I had never seen happen before, and haven't seen happen since: The pilot, which had not aired, received a rave write-up in *Details* magazine.

The next day, the pilot was picked up to series. We received an initial order of eight episodes (which was later expanded to thirteen episodes). An airdate for the pilot was set for April 15, 1990, almost a year since the original pilot was shot.

Fox announced the show somewhat safely as a "contemporary comedy-variety show."

Keenen continued to work on the show, picking those segments he thought would best showcase *In Living Color*'s unique take on contemporary culture.

Now that we were going to series, a production office was opened, on the fifth floor of a Fox building in Hollywood, with offices for the producers and writers. There was a communal kitchen, a conference room, and a gym, which Keenen got Fox to install. Downstairs were the offices for cast members, dancers, and the stage, where we would rehearse and film.

We had shot the pilot as an hour show. It would now be cut down to a half hour. HBO, which had financed the pilot, decided not to stay on for the series. Fox's Twentieth Television stepped up (although common now, it was more unusual at the time because of concerns about the conflicts of interest between financing a show and the network having the same ownership).

Despite claiming that they wanted to push the envelope, Peter Chernin, then a top Fox executive, felt that some of Keenen's original skits went too far—at least for the pilot. Chernin asked Keenen to hold back skits like "Men on Film," "The Wrath of Farrakhan," and "Homeboy Shopping Network" to later episodes (if indeed there were later episodes). Keenen refused.

Only Buddy Sheffield and Sandy Frank returned to write the series. Kevin Bright, who'd helped to produce the pilot, left the show. I had liked him tremendously, but the chemistry with Keenen just wasn't there, and it was Keenen's show. (Don't feel bad for Kevin. He went on to produce an NBC sitcom that did okay. It was called *Friends*.)

Rawitt then staffed the writers' room with two black stand-up comics that I knew from the Comedy Act, Franklyn Ajaye and Barry "Berry" Douglas. She hired two more Letterman writers, Matt Wickline and Joe Toplyn, and two female writers, Mimi Friedman and Jeanette Collins.

Keenen and Tamara decided that a half hour needed less cast members. Jeff Joseph, T.J., and Toney did not stay on for the series. A lot of the "meta" material making fun about the show itself went out the window. And DJ Daddy Mack was replaced by SW1, or Shawn Wayans as he was more commonly known, who wouldn't actually DJ, but needed to look like he was. But Shawn proved his value to the show by getting his friend Heavy D to do *In Living Color*'s iconic theme song.

On April 15, 1990, following an episode of the popular *Married with Children,* Fox premiered *In Living Color.* It was seen by more than 20 million viewers—very big numbers. It was an overnight sensation. The *Philadelphia Inquirer* called it "the fastest funniest half-hour in a long time." The *Columbus Dispatch* said the show "catapulted television back to the cutting edge." It was all anybody was talking about in Hollywood the next day.

I knew the show was popular, but I really was unprepared for my life changing. Shortly after the show premiered, I was doing a weekend gig at a comedy club in West Palm Beach. I stopped to buy some orange juice at a supermarket near the club . . . and suddenly the whole checkout line stopped. All the cashiers down the line were all looking at me, saying, "Look who's in the store!" That was the weirdest thing ever.

Actually, it wasn't. The weirdest thing that happened was a few weeks later when I was in New York for the weekend.

I was riding the subway to an appointment when the car filled up with high school kids. They started staring at me and then just started screaming and pressing around me. It was just a weird kind of claustrophobic feeling. I had to jump off at the next stop and take a cab to my destination.

I don't think I rode the subway for years after that.

Chapter 5

The First Season

How do I describe that first season? It wasn't like being in the eye of a hurricane, or riding a rocket ship to the moon. It was a bit like *A Hard Day's Night,* which is to say, you were always on: either trying to write a skit, get in a skit that the writers had come up with, or act in a skit. And like the Beatles in their early days, we lived, breathed, ate, and hung out with each other before, during, and after the show.

It was a bubble. An enormously creative bubble. But it was also like being in a snowball careening down a mountain, getting bigger all the time, but not realizing that, eventually, you might go *SPLAT*!

What was great about that first season, and even if you watch it now, is that you can see all the cast members doing what they did best and finding themselves in doing so. That was what was great about Keenen. He knew what he wanted. He knew where he wanted the show to go. But at the same time, he stood back and allowed the cast to take the characters, make them their own, and sometimes take those characters way, way out.

On the first show of *In Living Color* that ever aired, I appeared in the second skit of the show's history, "Great Moments in Black History: The First Black Man to Walk on the Moon."

Looking like a very serious PBS program, or a public service announcement, a PSA, the sketch opened with the silhouette of a row of men. As the lights came up, we saw a row of African-American men and women outlined as I stood before them in a dark suit and tie, looking sharp and professorial (and with a Fu-Manchu mustache!).

The conceit was that alongside Neil Armstrong, Buzz Aldrin, and Michael Collins, there was a black astronaut on board, Slick Johnson. However, after landing, Armstrong was informed there was only enough fuel to return three astronauts safely to Earth. So they sent Johnson to find a spot for volleyball and then left without him. The viewers saw an astronaut jumping on the moon and heard what was supposed to be Johnson saying, "C'mon, man!" Then I said, "The mission was otherwise a perfect success and an embarrassed NASA deleted all references to Slick Johnson." And I concluded with: "I'm Tommy Davidson with another great moment in black history." That was how America first got to know me.

During that first season, the cast became family. David Alan Grier, Jim Carrey, and I had each other's back. We were able to protect and take care of each other. The first-season cast included Kelly Coffield, T'Keyah Crystal Keymáh, and Kim Coles.

There's no denying that *In Living Color* was the Wayans Full Employment Act. During the course of the series, Keenen hired Damon, Kim, Shawn, and Marlon Wayans as cast members. Even Dwayne Wayans, who had little discernible acting talent, was hired as a production assistant and occasional extra.

By the way, Dwayne was my favorite because he re-
minded me of the guys I grew up with. He was thick as a
brick and twice as tough. You knew he did all the fighting.
We had this thing where we'd give each other a look—eye
to eye, man to man—because he understood where I came
from in a way the others didn't. And I got that what
Keenen and Damon had, he would never get, but Dwayne
was his own man. Dwayne and I also got along because he
loved and wrote music (his son is a music composer).

"James Carrey," or Jim as most of the world has come
to know him, had been a friend since we first met at the
Comedy Store. I was so grateful to be able to play with
Jim in such a creative way on *In Living Color*.

The audience saw Jim in the first sketch of the first
episode, "Love Connection," where Jim played Chuck
Woolery, and the two contestants were Mike Tyson (played
by Keenen) and Robin Givens (played by Kim Coles). That
first episode, and even the first few episodes, did not really
expose the full range of Jim's talent. For the most part, in
those first few skits, he played the white guy. He was a
child in the playground; he was Captain Kirk from *Star
Trek*.

You had to wait until episode four, broadcast on May 5,
1990, for "Jim Carrey Transition." (Transitions being scenes
that bridge you between two set pieces, such as rounds in a
boxing match, or sketches on a comedy show.) For Jim's
transition scene, it was just him, doing some of his you-
can't-believe-your-eyes contortions, first with his body
and then with his face, neck, and even throat, culminating
in one of his celebrity imitations (I think the first one was
Jack Nicholson).

It was really episode six, which aired on May 19, 1990,

where people became aware of the immensity of Jim's talent. The first sketch was "Bad Karate Class," where Jim was playing the teacher of a women's self-defense course. In it, he claimed to be a champion, but, instead, he ended up being stabbed and beaten by the women in his class. Doesn't sound funny when I describe it like that, but the way Jim pushed his character to extremes was very funny.

By the time Jim played Vera de Milo, in episode ten, the audience expected Jim to do crazy things with his body, but each time, he just topped them. In "Vera de Milo, Bodybuilder," Jim played this very masculine woman. The skit was making fun of female athletes on the East German and Russian teams who seemed more like men than women, and those athletes whose steroid use had made them freaks.

The scene opened up with the woman bodybuilder in silhouette, striking bodybuilding poses. You could see her pigtails and the outline of the body that made you think this was a real bodybuilder. Then the light came on and you saw it was Jim in this unitard, contorting his body in ways that made it seem like he was this bulked-up bodybuilder. It was absurd! You couldn't help but laugh, but there was something uncomfortable about it as well. That was a crazy-ass sketch.

With that one sketch, that was it: Jim was established as the guy who could do extreme characters and do extreme things with his face and his body. He would bend his body and contort himself in any way, shape, or form. He was Elastic Man.

One of the first scenes I did with Jim was "Jheri's Kids," which was also in episode six, where Jim played Jerry Lewis at his telethon. As the scene progressed, it turned out that the telethon is to benefit kids who suffered from Jheri curl syndrome and I was the kid with the Jheri curl activation problem. "Fight this Jheri curl syndrome." It was a funny concept, and Jim and I just lit it on fire. You see on the screen how much fun we were having.

Although I had known Jim for a while, it was wonderful to discover that when we were in a scene together, we were one mind. I got him and where he was going and then I sent it back to him. He got what I was about and what to do with it. It was a beautiful thang.

That was the thing about *In Living Color:* You could tell how sometimes the cast couldn't believe what they were getting away with.

Personally, that first season, one of the performers who was a revelation to me was Kelly Coffield (today she is known as Kelly Coffield Park). Like Jim, she was one of the few white cast members (there was one white male and one white female). Kelly just went to places you couldn't imagine her going—like playing Sam Kinison or doing a female Andrew Dice Clay.

Andrea Dice Clay may be one of the funniest bits I've ever seen. Kelly committed to that character and lived it and breathed it in a way that made you believe she could have done a full comedy set as Andrea Dice Clay. It just blew me away.

Kelly was tremendously talented. She and T'Keyah were from the Chicago comedy scene. She had a lily-white Illinois accent, but was just like us, crazy as shit. She could hang with us and didn't have any hang-ups about race. She was perfect for whatever sketch she was put up for. We were like the closest of closest partners on that first cast; we were the 1977 Pittsburgh Steelers. Watching this Midwestern white woman putting it all out there in sketches with black people from New York City and Washington, D.C., was just another example of how *In Living Color* split the atom in society.

Kelly and I had an amazing sketch that first season called "Endangered Species." It appeared in episode eight, but we had shot it earlier. It was held for being too edgy. And it was.

"Endangered Species" opened up on Jim sitting at the desk of *The Tonight Show,* announcing that he's Alan Thicke filling in for Johnny Carson (and, in typical Jim brilliance, there's an aside where he says, "Because everyone knows at this point another Johnny Carson impression would be totally passé."). Then he announces that his next guest is Joan Embery from the San Diego Zoo. At which point, Kelly comes out dressed in khaki safari shirt and shorts, carrying me on her back. That's right, *me.* She has a young black man on her back who is wearing a Kangol hat and sneakers. She explains that he is an endangered species: "He's Calvin, a homeboy sapiens africanus, or a B-boy."

I sat there, my arms crossed in front of me, and Jim asked Kelly, "What's he doing now?" She answered, "He's chillin'." This was all the more amazing, since it's 1990 and the rest of the country wouldn't be using the expression "chillin'" for about twenty years. We're basically introducing hip-hop culture to the mainstream with this one sketch. Chillin', even back then, right? Yeah, that's where it came from. Wasn't that shit great?

What I loved was that we were able to juxtapose the hip-hop world against the mainstream white world. This is exactly what *In Living Color* aspired to do: to make mainstream America realize hip-hop was worth celebrating.

David Alan Grier was probably the most talented among us. David was a Tony Award–nominated dramatic actor, who was also a graduate of Yale School of Drama. His father was a psychiatrist, and Grier and his father had marched with Martin Luther King Jr. in the streets of his native Detroit. David was a friend of both Robert Townsend's and Keenen's and had even had a part in Keenen's film.

David wasn't extreme like Jim. He was the slow burn; he could slay with a raised eyebrow. David's character Calhoun Tubbs, Blues Great, was a spot-on take on the clichés of a legendary bluesman. David would play, seated, and his character would claim to have written thousands of songs. However, each song said truths about the people around him that they would prefer not to hear. David played it straight and had every detail of the bluesman down, but the sheer outrageousness of what he said, and the reaction to it, made it so funny.

He could do characters of all sorts, and crazy shit would come out of his mouth when you least expected it. Still, he was solid, so often in a sketch, he acted like home base for the viewers, being the person they could see themselves in. Even when he was Antoine in "Men on Film."

Kim Wayans launched herself out of the gate with a parody of Tracy Chapman: "I write me a fast song." The sketch had her as Chapman, a very popular singer at the time, having to come up with a song, and doing it by just saying whatever she saw out the window of her own apartment. It was, in its own way, brilliant and, more important, it showed that *In Living Color* was not afraid to skewer other African Americans. There were no sacred cows on *In Living Color.*

Another of Kim's signature characters was Benita Butrell. Benita was a black woman in the neighborhood who gossiped about everything and knew everyone's business. She'd sit in the window and go, "You didn't hear this from me, but such and such down there is on heroin."

*   *   *

T'Keyah Crystal Keymáh found her spot in Black World with a scene she did for her audition where she played a young black girl speaking about her dreams of an imagined postracial world. It was devastating social commentary. Keenen was smart to make her part of the mix. She was a great person and we got along really well. We often rehearsed together. She would go on to be featured on *Cosby* and then would play Raven's mother in *That's So Raven*.

Kim Coles was another talent Keenen found in New York. I had known her from way back in the day when we both did amateur night at the Apollo. She was great at characters and accents. For the pilot, she played Robin Givens in the "Love Connection" sketch and knocked that out of the park.

As for me, I was in a number of great sketches that first season. In the second episode, I was given the opportunity to do a transition sketch. Mine was with David, and we played the tuxedo-wearing sports commentators at a boxing prizefight. I was doing my Sugar Ray Leonard impression, and the funny thing is that because you couldn't understand half of what I was saying, it was really, really funny.

I got to do Sugar Ray again in another sketch that got a huge reaction, "Three Champs and a Baby," which was the first sketch on episode five that aired on July 15, 1990. Sandy Frank, if I recall correctly, wrote "Three Champs and a Baby."

In 1987, there had been a very successful movie, *Three Men and a Baby*, which was about these three single men (Tom Selleck, Ted Danson, and Steve Guttenberg) forced to raise a child without any of them knowing exactly which one of them, or any of them, was the father. (In 1990, it spawned a sequel, *Three Men and a Little Lady*.)

In *In Living Color*'s version, Muhammad Ali (David), Mike Tyson (Keenen), and Sugar Ray Leonard (me) discover that they were all at the same party and all were with the same woman who has now left them a baby that may be one of theirs. It was a politically incorrect way to acknowledge the fact that many African-American professional athletes fathered children out of wedlock—and the joke was in making it seem as innocent and fun as a Disney movie.

That was an important sketch for me. Being one of those three with Keenen and David made me feel like I was part of the show's DNA. It was a good feeling—one I wouldn't always have on the show.

However, the sketch that made me seemed on paper like not much: a sketch about MC Hammer's pants. I had to wait until episode eleven of that first season, which aired on July 15, 1990, but, man, was it worth the wait!

Matt Wickline had pitched a sketch that was as simple as MC Hammer dancing and getting lost in his big-ass Aladdin-style harem pants, until, eventually, the pants get the best of him. Keenen recognized this was a perfect sketch for me. All Matt had to tell me was "Go!"

I had to talk, sing, and dance as MC Hammer—all of it at high speed—making fun of his lyrics. Then I had to come up with a way for those pants to take over. I knew that this one was a rocket ship and I was going to take it to the max.

What made the sketch pop was my dancing and all these precision spins that I did. God knows how I knew to do them, but I could—and still can! Watching it today, it's still surprising and spellbinding. You can't look away. And you can see the moment it hits you: Nobody else but Tommy Davidson could do that. I became the guy who could parody musical entertainers. I became the high-energy guy.

Credit for that goes to Keenen. Keenen allowed me to stand out in that way. Keenen was great at taking what we already had and then enhancing it. He would step back. If you had a character, and Keenen liked your character, he'd let you work on it with the writers; then he would come in at the end and fine-tune it.

Keenen was someone with a strong vision. He cast the show with several of these extreme talents (or rather talents who could perform extreme impersonations). Jim, Kelly, and I were in that category. We were supporting and surrounding a core of "normal" talent that was very funny, such as David, Kim Coles, Kim Wayans, and T'Keyah. Additionally, we were supporting Keenen and Damon, who could do "real" characters, play them straight and deadpan, in ways that were brilliant and that allowed them to say the most outrageous things. They could take it to places you never imagined (like "Men on . . ." or "Homey D. Clown" sketches) and take the audience with them.

Keenen was smart in that he didn't play us off each other as a competition; he allowed our very different talents to play off each other in the scene to produce better television.

One of my favorite sketches that first season was "Don King, The Early Years." What at first seemed like an episode of *Our Gang,* with kids about to fight in the schoolyard, changed when a Buckwheat-looking figure, played by Damon, appeared as the fight's referee. This tipped us off that this was a Don King biopic, with Don's wild hair and fight-impresario style already in evidence.

Another of the sketches that first year that stuck was the "Hey Mon" sketches about a West Indian family and their superhuman work ethic. Franklin Ajaye wrote the sketch, but all the other writers, including John Bowman and

Sandy Frank, added gags and punched it up. If I remember right, "Hey Mon" was originally written for David Alan Grier, but in rehearsal he couldn't do a Jamaican accent. It sounded more like a leprechaun. So David gave the sketch to Damon. And Damon killed it. And the day after, and ever since, you'd be hearing people saying, "Hey, mon."

I played one of the kids on that. T'Keyah, Kim, and Keenen were all part of the "Hey Mon" sketches, along with Damon, all of us in dreadlocks, talking about all these jobs we were holding. That woke up the whole Caribbean community in relation to the black community. This was a big stew we were making. And Keenen was fearless, he wanted us to dive right in.

Keenen gave us the freedom to just riff in character. That was our sketch: "Hey, mon, I can't go to do that job today, because I got the laundry. Then I got to go over to the grocery store and bag, then I got to hit the trash truck in the mornin' and go and empty the trash. Then I got to go to IHOP and make three thousand pancakes, and then . . . Hey, mon, got to go to work."

"Hey Mon" doesn't sound like much, but it was huge. Every Caribbean person in the world identified with that sketch.

One of the most famous sketches that people talk about to this day was "Homey D. Clown."

In the sketch that introduced Homey, I was the kid whose birthday party Homey was performing at. Homey was an ex-con whose probation forced him to take the job of clown, but he wouldn't do anything that he felt debased or insulted him. "Homey may be a clown, but he don't make a fool out of himself" was how he put it in that first sketch. As each kid (played by David, Kelly, T'Keyah, and me) suggested Homey do something funny (slip on a banana peel, get a cream pie in the face), he told them, "I don't think so. Homey don't play that."

There are many different versions of how that sketch came to be. Most involve a comic genius who deserves to be better known and get more props than he does, because he is truly one of the greats, Paul Mooney. Take a look at any of the greatest black comedians and you will find that they have one thing in common: They worked with Paul.

Mooney was born in Shreveport, Louisiana, and grew up in Oakland, California. His grandmother who raised him gave him the nickname of Mooney. Per Wikipedia, it was because of actor Paul Muni in *Scarface*. I always thought it was his given last name, but I learned that was Gladney.

As a young man, Mooney actually ran off to join the circus, working as a ringmaster with the Gatti-Charles Circus. During this time, he started writing and performing jokes. He wrote for *Sanford and Son*, and then wrote for Richard Pryor's appearance on *Saturday Night Live* (Pryor insisted on using his own writer). He was a writer credited on the two single greatest filmed comedy performances, *Richard Pryor: Live in Concert* and *Richard Pryor: Live on the Sunset Strip*. His acting credits go from *The Buddy Holly Story* (where he played Sam Cooke) to appearing on *Chappelle's Show* and having his own show, *Judge Mooney*.

Paul Mooney did not fraternize with the other writers or even the other cast members. More to the point, Mooney didn't fraternize. He was just angry all the time. That was his stock in trade.

Here's what Damon told the Uproxx website in 2015 about Homey and Paul Mooney: "Paul Mooney, he was the angriest black man in the world and he prided himself on that. Like, he wouldn't even pitch ideas for sketches in front of white people. 'Not in front of the white people,

Homey. One on one, me and you, Keenen, and I'll tell you everything. Not in front of the white people.' And he would say, 'Homey,' you know. 'Homey this, Homey that. Oh, Homey, Homey. Not in front of the white people, Homey.' So this guy, Sandy Frank—these are writers—and Matt Wickline said, 'You know, this is funny. The clown who won't perform.' So they wrote Homey D. Clown and I put the angry black man voice on Homey D. Clown, because I just thought it was appropriate, and the rest is history."

Matt Wickline was actually the one who pitched Damon on the idea of an angry clown. Keenen and Damon immediately jumped on it and thought it was hysterical, and Damon was like, "I'm doing this!" Keenen asked Matt to work with Damon on it. According to Matt, Damon right away had the voice for Homey. It was a specific hard guy, but said in Damon's high-pitched voice. According to Matt, at one of the readings, Shawn was laughing so hard and said, "Homey don't play." Matt didn't know what he meant. But Damon just said it in that tight voice of his, "Homey don't play that." And that became the punch line.

Paul Mooney wasn't even a writer on the pilot. He was only hired halfway into the first season. And even then, his office wasn't with the other writers. No one really saw him at work, except for the rare occasion when he would show up at the writers' table to sound off about other people's sketches.

To play Homey D. Clown, Damon may well have been inspired by Paul Mooney to make the angry clown a black militant. As to who came up with "Homey don't play that," I have a slightly different recollection. It was during the sketch rehearsal for Homey. Damon hit me on the head with the sock and said, "Now, what you gotta say about that?" And I went: "Homey don't play that," and everybody just died laughing. Why did I say it just then? Was it because I had heard Mooney say it? Or did I hear Shawn say it? I can't tell you. But what I know is this: It was an ad-lib that worked, and the writers took it and ran with it. That little phrase that came out of my mouth became a national catchphrase. Homey don't play that, you know what I mean?

One more thing about Homey. My mother was not a fan. Remember, I played the little boy that he always hit over the head with the sock. My mom didn't like that. She would say to me, "Why do they always have to be hitting you?" She was pissed. I would tell her that it was okay. I was fine with it. It was comedy. It was TV.

But today, looking back, I admit she had a point. If they keep writing parts for you where you are the victim, the punching bag, chances are they are not, and never will be, your biggest fans. I understand that now. At the time, I was just happy to be in the sketch.

As for Damon, sometimes he dug deep for his characters. A good example of that is Handi-Man, a character he created who is a superhero for the handicapped who is severely handicapped himself.

The "Handi-Man" sketch had what, today, would be a politically incorrect setup. (It was politically incorrect then, too, and that's why the writers liked it.) At the annual dinner of the Legion of Superheroes, Jim, as a Superman-like character, announced that to settle a discrimination lawsuit against the Legion, they had to accept more diverse superheroes. Their new members were a Jewish superhero, Super Beard (a Hasidic-looking superhero), an Asian superhero, the Human Computer (exploiting the awful stereotype about Asians and math), the Angry Black Lesbian Superhero (who had brought the suit), and, finally, Handi-Man, a handicapped superhero to help the disabled.

Handi-Man had trouble speaking and his hands were deformed, as well as his legs. However, when the handicapped sign was projected on the clouds at night, that was his call to action. The crisis turned out to be about a handicapped person in a wheelchair (played by me) and a handicapped stall that had been occupied by a non-handicapped person. Handi-Man ripped the door off and confronted the non-handicapped person. The sketch ended with me expressing my gratitude for there finally being a superhero for the handicapped.

Despite all that, and all the politically incorrect humor, Damon had a very personal experience that informed the sketch. Damon explained on Uproxx: "I was born with a club foot and I used to talk about it onstage; you've got to turn the camera on yourself. So I decided, 'I'm gonna start talking about my club foot and the pain of having this, you know, orthopedic shoe that I had to wear as a kid.' The joke that started Handi-Man was I was saying I got into a lot of fights as a kid, because I had to defend my shoe. And I said, 'I guess you don't find too many handicapped bullies.' And then I would tell a little bit about, like, 'Uh-oh, here come the Crips,' and you have these handicapped guys roll up and go [standard un-PC mentally disabled voice] 'Give me your lunch money.' So that was the birth of Handi-Man, and then talking about how it's like they need a superhero. You never find a handicapped superhero. And then I start doing Handi-Man onstage."

Although Keenen did so much behind the scenes (supervising the writing and how the sketches were performed, the look of the show, and the Fly Girls) and introduced each episode, he still managed to appear in many, many memorable sketches. Perhaps my favorite that first season was Keenen's take on Little Richard. True to Little

Richard's reputation, Keenen played him taking credit for the invention of everything. It was spot-on and hilarious.

Probably, "Men on . . ." has become the most enduring sketch of the entire series. That sketch was another thing that just took the roof off the sucker. And give Keenen credit: It was the last sketch on the first episode. There was plenty of pressure to hold it back until later in the season. But Keenen said no. "Men on . . ." was ON!

The "Men on . . ." premise was simple: It was a Siskel & Ebert or Leonard Maltin–type review program, with two hosts, Blaine Edwards (Damon Wayans) and Antoine Merriweather (David Alan Grier), who were flamboyantly gay. The two characters saw the gay in everything. Sandy Frank, who wrote the sketch, didn't want it to be a sketch about gay film reviewers. What he thought was funny was that they saw the whole world as gay. That was what made the "Men on . . ." sketches hilarious.

Men on Films was billed as a public-access program in which films were reviewed "from a male point of view." The lead-in music was Paul Schaffer and the Weather Girls' "It's Raining Men." The curtain opened to reveal Blaine wearing a shirt whose buttons were all open and a little silk neckerchief tied around his throat and some kind of small hat on his bald head.

I can tell you that people were laughing before they ever said a word. And I mean the cast and crew as well. If you listen closely, you can hear Rosie Perez, who has one of the great laughs in the world, cackling in the background.

On *Men on Film,* a review of *Karate Kid III* summarized the film as "men working out their problems in a very physical way," and Antoine said Ralph Macchio's performance could be summed up in three words: "Fab. U. Lous." When Blaine disagreed with Antoine, Blaine pouted. The sponsors were products such as "Gaytorade" and "Bendgay."

So just saying a film title such as *Great Balls of Fire* took on a whole other meaning when Antoine said it. Another of their trademark bits was that if a film was all about women, they would dismiss it: "*Pretty Woman* . . . hated it!" But if there was a male or possible gay connotation to the title, they raved. So when they did *Men on Books,* they rated *Little Women* as "hated it!" But *Moby Dick* . . . you get the idea!

The "Men on . . ." characters would top off their reviews with their signature hand gesture, "two snaps," in its endless variations (two snaps up here; two snaps, a circle, a twist, and a kiss; two snaps in a Z formation, etc.). The "Men on . . ." bits took on a life of its own. "Two snaps" passed right into the culture.

David Alan Grier tells a funny story that his agent kept calling, saying, "They're doing two snaps at Columbia." Then he'd call again, "They're doing two snaps at Paramount. This is going to be huge!"

This was airing at a time when the image of the black male was still very macho, and homosexuality among the African-American community was still somewhat taboo, kept on the down low. The "Men on . . ." sketches rushed in where others feared to tread. As an interesting side note, it's important to remember that Damon Wayans was let go from *Saturday Night Live* for going off-script and making a character flamboyantly gay.

No question, it was the writers who made *In Living Color* as funny and as boundary-breaking as it was. Let me name them before I forget: Pam Veasey (head writer), Greg Fields (head writer), Les Firestein (head writer), Keenen Ivory Wayans, Fax Bahr, Fred Graver, Adam Small, Michael

Anthony Snowden, Steve Tompkins, Damon Wayans, Larry Wilmore, Marc Wilmore, Harry Dunn, Michelle Jones, Becky Hartman Edwards, Buddy Sheffield, John Bowman, Mimi Friedman, Jeanette Collins, Sandy Frank, and Matt Wickline.

The way Keenen had set it up was that the writers would pitch him on Monday, and then the writers would get assignments from that. But Keenen was tough. First of all, he didn't laugh or barely smiled when you pitched him. Sometimes, Jim or David would say, we've got a couple of ideas we want to kick around. And sometimes the Monday pitches didn't yield enough material that Keenen approved, so there would be a second pitch on Thursday.

In Living Color represented a progressive shift in television. It represented the most African Americans appearing together on television *not* playing a sport and without a ball. It was a new paradigm for comedy and we rode that train early. In no time, *In Living Color* quickly became a cultural touchstone, one of those shows where we'd do a sketch and the next day everyone was talking about it. It was "watercooler TV," before anyone coined that phrase.

Being on *In Living Color* was like being in a repertory troupe. You never knew from week to week what you were going to play. At the same time, Keenen allowed us to make the most out of even the smallest role. That was the challenge: to stand out even when you were in a background part. Put David Alan Grier in a small role and even he didn't know what kind of crazy shit was going to come out of his mouth. Keenen let the cameras roll and picked the best takes.

I caught on quickly that the writers were as competitive as the actors: They all wanted Keenen to choose their skit, and they wanted to write for those performers that Keenen favored. Similarly, as actors, we wanted to befriend and be adopted by those writers who were getting the most skits on air. It was like NFL training camp.

As an actor, the challenge was: What could you bring to the material? How could you add extra value? Was there an idea you could take and flip it on its ass? Was there a way to do the scene differently that made the scene funnier? Because what you didn't want to do was go for the funny just for the sake of looking good and upstaging another cast member. That was definitely not cool, and it would lead to other actors not working with you. The trick—and it was a difficult one—was to contribute something that was funny but made the other actors in the scene look good and that shone more glory on *In Living Color.*

So, for example, if there was a scene where I was a bank teller and someone was going to rob the bank, I might do my scene in an Indian accent. The idea was to have fun with it. In the long run, that was what saved me on the show. You couldn't put me far back enough in the sketch, because something I would say would stay with you after the sketch was done.

A good example was a sketch we had first season we called "Snackin' Shack," written by Mimi Friedman and Jeanette Collins, which was set in a black-run soul restaurant that was just nasty. This was before restaurants had to carry health grades in the window, but if they did, this one would be a D. In the sketch, I was in the kitchen and I'd do this whole thing where I'd go, "Pick it up, pick it up, pick it up." That became part of the sketch.

Here's a little bit of *In Living Color* trivia. If you look at the "Snackin' Shack" scenes, you will notice Tom Joyner, the radio personality, is in one of them.

Here's why: Back in the day before I got the show, when I was working at the deli and doing the comedy shows, I also wrote jokes for Tom. I got paid something like thirty dollars a pop for a bit—and back then, that money made a difference in my life and that of my family. So, once the show was on the air, I contacted him and he flew out to L.A. and did a cameo on *In Living Color.*

In Living Color's success wasn't only because of the sketches and the actors. Another big part of the show was the Fly Girls. From the very beginning, Keenen had this idea that his show would feature hip-hop dancers and a DJ rather than a house band. If *SNL* had the Blues Brothers, we had the Fly Girls. They set the tone and communicated that this was a hip-hop show. That this was hip-hop nation.

The Fox presentation pilot and the original Fly Girls were choreographed by A.J. Johnson. By the time the series was ordered, she had been offered a role in the Kid 'n Play movie *House Party.* Keenen was looking for another choreographer when his casting director, Robi Reed, suggested Rosie Perez.

Rosie was an amazing force of nature. She's written her own story, *Handbook for an Unpredictable Life,* and it is truly worth reading. Although I didn't know it at the time, we have more in common than I ever knew regarding how our childhood traumas affected our anger and behavior. Post-traumatic stress disorder (PTSD) in childhood creates triggers in adult life. But when I met her, Rosie was an amazing bundle of energy.

Rosie had moved out to L.A. from Brooklyn when she was nineteen (around 1983 or 1984). She had spent her childhood between Brooklyn and upstate New York, between being a ward of the state and attending a Catholic convent school, and having to deal with her own family traumas. But she knew she was special and that her talent was meant to be shared with a larger world.

Rosie was living with family out here and attending college, where she was studying biochemistry. She used to go to the clubs in L.A. and dance up a storm. She was discovered and asked to be a *Soul Train* dancer. On YouTube, you can watch a compilation of her appearances. You can see a lot of moves that she would bring to *In Living Color,* as well as some moves that were so ahead of their time that they are only making it to the dance floor now.

When she was on *Soul Train,* Rosie did this type of dancing called "face dancing," which is where your face is fierce and almost separate from the moves your body is making. And when you watch Rosie in those *Soul Train* performances, you can see the anger inside her, and the ferocious fierceness and drive that animated her.

In 1988, dancing her ass off in another L.A. club called Funky Reggae, she was approached by Spike Lee, who asked her to read for *Do the Right Thing.* Although Rosie assumed Spike was just coming on to her (and he may have been), he did cast her as Tina, the girlfriend and baby mama of Lee's character. And Rosie made *Do the Right Thing*'s credits most memorable by dancing throughout them.

Robi Reed, who had been Keenen's casting director on *I'm Gonna Git You Sucka,* was also casting director on *In Living Color.* Robi had worked on Spike Lee's *Do the Right Thing* and suggested Rosie to Keenen. Keenen met with her and wanted to make her an offer. But before he could, she took a job as choreographer for the dancers for LL Cool J's tour. Keenen hired another choreographer, Carla Earle, but Keenen quickly felt she wasn't delivering his vision. When LL Cool J performed in L.A., Keenen went to see Perez and made her an offer. With LL's blessing, she did not refuse. Rosie was hired.

Although Rosie had been living in L.A., Rosie was Brooklyn. Rosie knew her hip-hop moves from New York, Brooklyn, and the Bronx. Equally important, she had learned to choreograph routines by being on the cheerleading squad at her school in upstate New York. This was the winning combination Keenen needed.

As Rosie once explained, "Keenen had enough faith in me to bring hip-hop to the mass media. I love dance and I really wanted to let the world in on that culture, and I wanted it so bad to be authentic."

She brought hip-hop style to L.A. However, a lot of the dancers didn't know hip-hop dancing and the moves that Rosie wanted them to do.

For the dancers, Deidre Lang and Carrie Ann Inaba among them, Rosie didn't speak in the jazz or modern dance or ballet vocabulary, so they had a hard time understanding and communicating with Rosie. That sometimes meant ten- to twelve-hour days to learn Rosie's moves. Each week, it took four days to learn the dances and work with whatever other talent was brought in. It was not easy and Rosie was really tough on them.

On the website Mental Floss, Rosie said in a quoted article, "I remember going up to Keenen's office like, 'They hate me!' . . . Keenen said, 'Just do your job.'" And she did.

All Rosie and the dancers' efforts paid off big. The Fly Girls became a sorority with its own fan base. People tuned in to see what they would do each week.

That first season, no one was safe. We made fun of Paul Reubens getting caught in an adult theater, in "Pee-wee's Porn House." We made fun of the movie *Misery*, with Kelly doing the Kathy Bates role. We took on Louis Farrakhan in two different sketches. The first, "The Wrath of Farrakhan," which I mentioned earlier, was balls-out brilliant.

It's not like Keenen didn't know that Farrakhan had made anti-Semitic or Holocaust-denying statements. It's not like Keenen didn't know that the mere sight of a Farrakhan character on network TV would offend Jewish entertainment-industry agents, executives, and attorneys. It was Keenen's perverse way of saying that African Americans perceived Farrakhan differently, as someone who, despite saying offensive things, also spoke truths others didn't want to hear, but needed to be said. By calling the sketch, "The Wrath of Farrakhan," and comparing him to a *Star Trek* villain, Keenen made it okay to have a sketch about him.

The other Farrakhan sketch was a version of the classic Abbott and Costello routine "Who's on First," reimagined for Al Sharpton and Farrakhan. Not as funny, but even more transgressive. These were sketches you could never imagine being done on *SNL* or anywhere else for that matter. That was Keenen. He was not afraid to "boldly go where no man has gone before."

Perhaps our most outrageous sketch—way ahead of the curve on this one—was our Macaulay Culkin–Michael Jackson sketch, "Home Alone Again." It's so crazy, I thought I'd quote some of the dialogue. A very young Jonathan Taylor Thomas, who would go on to continued fame on shows like *Home Improvement* and *Last Man Standing,* and who voiced young Simba in *The Lion King,* played Macaulay. I played Michael.

The sketch opened with Culkin on his staircase inside his home as the announcer said, "Macaulay Culkin is at it again. But this time . . ." The camera cuts to me as Michael Jackson, crouching outside the door, trying to peer in the mail slot, as the announcer continues, "He's home alone again, with Michael Jackson."

The scene was really fierce: It focused on Michael Jackson's behaviors that more than once seemed to cross the line. We had Michael sending Culkin's parents to the Bahamas in order to be alone with him. Michael tried to entice Culkin to let him in the house, saying, "I'll let you play with one of my old noses." Culkin asked Michael if he was going to dump him, like he did with child star Webster. Michael offered naked pictures of his sister. I did all my Michael dance moves. I had been doing Michael for so many years in my stand-up act that it all came naturally to me.

Finally the scene ended when Culkin let Michael inside the house, only to set Michael's hair on fire. Michael responded: "What is this, the Pepsi commercial?" Michael suggested they should head to his house, where they could play with the Elephant Man or nap in his oxygen chamber.

This was when the announcer said: "*Home Alone Again,* coming this season."

That was genius.

Now, two things I'd like to add about that sketch. First, you may be wondering how we got some of those jokes by the censors. Because there was always an executive from Fox on the set, looking over the script, listening to what we said, watching what we did. And ready to shut us down.

But here's the thing: They didn't understand half of what we said, because either we were doing a voice, or we were talking so fast, or they were not hip to the language we were using. So shit sailed right by, all the time. Also, there was so much taboo-busting material that they couldn't keep up. If they focused on one thing, five more sailed through. That, too, was Keenen. "Do what you do," Keenen said, "I'll handle the censors." And Keenen and Tamara did. Again and again.

The second thing about the *Home Alone* parody was that it established that Michael Jackson was a character

Tommy Davidson could do. And I did. On more than one occasion.

We knew we were making something special. Audiences agreed. The show was regularly in the top ten, which, for a Fox show, was unheard of. We were scoring some 18 million viewers a week.

Jim would come into the room where we hung out, saying, "This is history. This is going to go down in history as this important show." And no one argued with him. We all felt that way.

In Living Color was the right show, at the right time, on the right network. It found an audience that allowed each of us involved in the show to demonstrate our talents. Keenen had a real sense of excellence and he really pushed us to achieve it. A lot of us were built to respond to that.

Jim always used to say that *In Living Color* was a giant door that we were lucky enough to all walk through.

We ended that first thirteen-episode season strong. Our second-to-last sketch that season was Kelly's scorching take on a female Sam Kinison, Samantha Kinison. If you've never seen it, it is worth playing. Kelly takes no prisoners. It is all-out commitment. It was so good that like John Belushi doing his Joe Cocker imitation beside Cocker on-stage, or Jimmy Fallon doing Bruce Springsteen or Neil Young next to them, Kelly eventually got to do a scene as Samantha Kinison with the real Sam Kinison. And if watching that doesn't blow your mind, I don't know what will.

And the last sketch was "The Buttmans," a traditional sitcom about a family whose heads are butts. Jim played Richard Dickerson, whose nose was a *dick*! And the punch line was "Who would ever imagine our daughter dating a white guy?" "The Buttmans" became a running series of sketches. That episode aired on September 9, 1990.

A week later, on Sunday, September 16, 1990, the 42nd Primetime Emmy Awards were held at the Pasadena Civic Auditorium in Pasadena, California, which aired on Fox. That year, the Emmys were hosted by Candice Bergen, Jay Leno, and Jane Pauley.

In Living Color was nominated for four Emmys. We had barely been on the air for five months and were already being nominated for awards! That was crazy.

Sandy Frank was nominated for "Outstanding Writing in a Variety or Music Program" for the pilot episode. Rosie was nominated for her choreography. And the show itself was nominated for "Outstanding Variety, Music, or Comedy Series."

It was an amazing night—a legendary evening. Awards were given to Peter Falk for *Columbo;* Candice Bergen won her second Emmy for *Murphy Brown;* Ted Danson won for *Cheers;* Patricia Wettig for *Thirtysomething;* Jimmy Smits for *L.A. Law*; and Marg Helgenberger for *China Beach*. This year was also memorable because in three award categories the Emmy voters granted a tie. That had never happened before or since.

Peter Falk gave one of the funniest speeches I'd ever heard, saying, "It's wonderful to win. I'm trying to find some way to be humble . . . but it's not going to work." He was very funny.

For me to be in that room with all that talent was crazy. Just a few years ago I was working in a kitchen in Maryland. Not so many months before I was still working at the deli.

At the same time, to be honest, it was a pretty white room. If you think the Oscars are so white now, imagine the Emmys in 1990. Just about the only people with yellow skin on the program were the Simpsons, who presented an award through the magic of animation. The *In Living*

Color seats in the auditorium, along with *Arsenio*'s, were pretty much the diversity in the room. The great director Thomas Carter, one of the few African-American directors at the time, was the tie winner with Scott Winant. Carter won for directing *Equal Justice*, so that makes one-half African-American winners at the 1990 Emmys. Jimmy Smits was the sole Latino.

The Fly Girls performed at the Emmys, showing their combination of acrobatics and dance moves. They brought hip-hop to what might have been the least hip audience they'd ever been in front of.

Rosie didn't win. Neither did Sandy.

And then they announced the category of "Outstanding Variety, Music, or Comedy Series." *In Living Color* was up against *Arsenio Hall, Late Night with David Letterman, Saturday Night Live,* and *The Tracey Ullman Show.*

They announced, "*In Living Color.*" Time stopped. We all wondered if we'd heard right.

Then the room exploded in applause and Keenen was making his way to the stage.

Keenen, looking sharp in his tuxedo, nonetheless seemed completely caught off guard. He was so overwhelmed by the moment he could barely talk. He started by thanking his family, saying, "They are the ones I been doing this for," and then he had to stop. He said to himself, "All right, let me chill." As he recalled at a later date, "I was overwhelmed because I had never won anything. To win something, and for this to be the first thing that I won, was overwhelming." Keenen mentioned that his parents were in the audience and the camera cut to them. Keenen was about to talk when the music played him off. So Keenen held the statue aloft and, as he walked offstage, said, "This is for you, Mom."

*　　*　　*

You couldn't imagine a better topper to the first season: winning "Outstanding Variety, Music, or Comedy Series" in our first at bat. It was just incredible.

By this time, my career was exploding in ways I could have never imagined. At the same time, though, I was also playing with dynamite that would eventually make my career that much harder.

But first, I had to star in a movie with a young actress who'd gotten a lot of attention playing a crack addict in a Spike Lee film: Halle Berry.

Chapter 6

Keeping It Strictly Business

Getting the leading role in the movie *Strictly Business*, which was to film during our shooting hiatus in 1990, after the first season of *In Living Color*, was the greatest thing that had happened to my career, up to that point.

Way back when, Sinclair Jones had laid out a three-part plan for our success: First was to make a name for myself in the comedy world. We had done that when I headlined in the Main Room at the Comedy Store. The next step was TV, and when *In Living Color* was a success, it was time to focus on phase three: being a success in film. I had every hope that *Strictly Business* would be the key to that.

Chris Zarpas, the Disney executive who introduced me to my agent, Cary Woods, knew about this script that Mark Burg wanted to produce. Burg was running the film division of Island, Chris Blackwell's company. I no longer recall whether he told me about the project or told Mark about me, but my agent told me they were interested in me for a leading part. Robi Reed, who cast *In Living Color* (and pretty much cast anything that meant anything in

Black World), was casting the film and she recommended me as well.

The *Strictly Business* script was written by the up-and-coming journalist Nelson George. He proved to be a multitalented wordsmith and all-around Renaissance man. I loved hanging out with Nelson. He was a true intellectual, and I was impressed that he'd been published all over the place.

The premise of *Strictly Business* was pretty simple: Joseph C. Phillips played Waymon, a BUPPIE who's in the real estate business and has a long-term girlfriend he's not excited by. When he meets Halle Berry's Natalie, he falls in love with her. Here's the Cyrano part: To romance her, he gets advice from my character, Bobby, a smooth operator, who works in Waymon's company mail room.

Although *Strictly Business* was a light romantic comedy, it did have something to say about the African-American experience in America. First of all, it is important to note that we filmed in Harlem. Not the Harlem of today, with multimillion-dollar apartments and can't-get-into restaurants, but in 1991, Harlem was down on its heels.

Second, let's not skip over that this was a movie written, directed, produced, and starring African Americans. This is something people are still fighting to do today—no matter what you hear about *Black Panther*. The central premise of the movie is about black men trying to make it in white corporate America. It examines the forces that hold them down, sabotage them, as well as their own complicated feelings about being an Uncle Tom or an Oreo or having bougie dreams. Finally this was a movie about African Americans working in the corporate world, with business ambitions—members of the rising black middle class. There had not been a lot of that on screen before. Or since.

Looking back, I like to say that what I loved about the

script and making the film was that it was a science-fiction movie. The science fiction was that it was all about an African-American–owned bank that was a major financial institution for the black middle class. That's a fantasy. And a black businessman seeking advice from a black street kid? When has that ever happened?

Andre Harrell was one of the producers and that meant set visits from Russell Simmons and Irving Azoff. The movie's writer Nelson George was a producer as well, and he had all the press connections. The movie was directed by Kevin Hooks (stepson of my aunt Rosie) and also produced by Mark Burg (who would go on to make a fortune from *Two and a Half Men* and Charlie Sheen). Filming in New York meant set visits from everyone from Bruce Willis to Denzel Washington.

Plus my supporting cast included some soon-to-be-famous talent: a great actor, a bit older, named Sam Jackson, who's known today as Samuel Jackson, and a young Isaiah Washington. Sam Jackson was wonderful to work with. He was such a pleasure to be with; you knew he would have a bright future. In later films, like *Pulp Fiction,* he would go on to show the world his serious acting chops. Same for Isaiah Washington, who was a beautiful human being.

I had Kim Coles (from *In Living Color*) to back me up. I also had Joseph C. Phillips. So I was good. Phillips is a smart, talented guy, and he had been on *The Cosby Show* for several seasons as Lieutenant Martin Kendall. Later on, he would become a conservative radio host and Christian talk show commentator, but that was still in his future. On this set, we were both trying to figure out our place in the movie business.

My costar and love interest? A TV actress making one of her first screen appearances, Halle Berry. Halle was every bit as beautiful then as she is now, maybe more so, because she really wasn't Halle Berry yet. She had done some TV series, but she wasn't that well-known or that confident about her acting. And she had all kinds of suitors paying court to her, everyone from Wesley Snipes to Clifton Davis.

Now, a bit about my PA. I was assigned a production assistant—a PA—a young kid who very much wanted to be in the business. His job was to pick me up every morning and drive me to the set. We got to be pretty friendly. He was working as an intern at a music company and so would take me out at nights to these underground hip-hop clubs in New York. That was where I got to be friends with Heavy D. This was also where I first saw acts that hadn't broken yet, but would go on to become famous, such as Busta Rhymes and A Tribe Called Quest.

He was a sweet kid. He looked like the bird in the Cocoa Puffs commercial. That's why everyone called him "Puffy." That's right, Sean "Puffy" Combs, P. Diddy. Diddy was my PA.

One morning when Puffy dropped me off at the set, he found himself blocked in by one serious-looking Teamster goombah. Puffy asked him to move. Words escalated to shouts, shouts to fists, and Puffy opened up a gash above the Teamster's eye. The Teamster called the police (imagine that, a Teamster goombah calling the police) and Puffy was arrested.

I didn't know any of that. I had gone to the set and my trailer to prepare for that day's scenes. In the meantime, Puffy was making his way through central booking. Did anyone on the production rush to bail Puffy out of jail? Did they send their attorney? Did Andre Harrell or Russell Simmons bail him out? No, they did not, because at four in the morning, I got a call from Puffy in jail telling me what had gone down and asking for my help.

I went down to the police station on Fourteenth Street. I told the desk sergeant about the movie, where it was being shot, and that I was one of the stars. I told him about Puffy and what a good kid he was and how much I needed him as my PA. The police officer, to his credit, released Puffy on his own recognizance. Puffy never forgot that I came for him when he called, no questions asked, and got him out of jail. Many years later, he hired me to come to Miami and perform at one of his events.

Back to Halle. Halle Berry was born in Cleveland, the daughter of a white mother and a black father. She was not just a beauty, but a beauty pageant winner. She won Miss Teen All American in 1985 and Miss Ohio USA in 1986. She was the first runner-up in the 1986 Miss USA pageant. She was the first African-American Miss World entrant in 1986, too.

Halle was hired for the film by the original director and two days later was fired. As Halle explained in an Arsenio Hall appearance, the director felt that she was too light-skinned. He hated that the love-interest roles in African-American movies always went to a light-skinned actor. They actually hired another actress, Adrienne-Joi "A.J." Johnson. However, they couldn't make up their mind about her. Soon the director was fired.

Kevin Hooks was then hired, and he rehired Halle.

Kevin was one of my idols. As an actor, he had played Morris Thorpe in *The White Shadow* TV show. He also appeared in *Sounder,* one of the most important movies made by African Americans, where he got to act with Cicely Tyson. Kevin also costarred in Gordon Parks Jr.'s last film, *Aaron Loves Angela,* in 1975.

Eventually Halle would win an Oscar for her incredible performance in *Monster's Ball,* but back then, she really wanted and needed to work on every scene. Kevin tasked me with rehearsing her. We would go over each of our scenes together and she basically moved into my trailer in those first weeks of the shoot.

Now let me make this clear: NOTHING HAPPENED BETWEEN US! I can't really say if it might have, or could have, or would have. All I know is that it didn't. I liked her and she liked me, but we each had our insecurities and our baggage.

I wasn't divorced from my wife, Desiree, but we were apart and I no longer wanted to be with her. But I wasn't going to cheat on her. I didn't want to be *that* guy.

There was something else. My wife, Desiree, and Halle had been roommates during the Miss Teen All American beauty contest and Desiree didn't like Halle. Desiree was constantly bad-mouthing her. And I knew Halle didn't like Desiree, either.

Here's the thing: I should have told Halle from the get-go that I was married to Desiree Keating. I should have brought it up right away. But I didn't. I couldn't bring myself to; I had a lot of reasons. Halle was my costar, and she was my love interest on screen. I didn't want our on-screen relationship to be tainted by her off-screen history with Desiree.

However, the more time went by, and the closer I became with Halle, the more I should have told her, and the more I couldn't.

The day came when I couldn't take it anymore. I was sitting with Halle in the cafeteria and she said to me: "Why are you still with a woman that you want to leave?" And in my mind, what I heard was: *"When you could be with someone who likes you and that you like, like me?"*

So I told her. I told her I was married to—*still married to*—Desiree Keating. I guess I was right to be afraid to tell, because Halle didn't say anything.

She stood up, walked out of the cafeteria, and we were never the same.

After that, I saw Halle on a few occasions, but there was no longer any trace of the friendship we had shared. She would be cordial, but it was as if a door inside her heart had closed, and there was no more room for me. To this day, it's as if she has forgotten working on that film together. This is ironic, because you could say that today if we meet, it's *Strictly Business*.

Chapter 7

The Second Season

After our first season's ratings and Emmy success, Fox was now an enthusiastic supporter of the program. They increased the order for the second season to twenty-six episodes and they increased the budget. But having to shoot twice as many sketches as the first season meant a lot more work. A lot more.

The secret to the high quality per sketch on *In Living Color* was that we shot many more sketches than aired. Because we were not a live show, Keenen could edit and cherry-pick the best sketches and sequence them in ways that made sense for each show. That's why many sketches we shot during season one appeared in season two, and some never appeared at all.

There was another secret to our success. The whole cast was on-set when we taped the sketches. We're all standing there just off-screen. In between takes, we would all run in and make suggestions, "Try this, try that." It was like being at a football game.

Also, when we performed our sketches, there was an audience—and between our sketches, we showed them the pretaped sketches. Keenen recorded the audience's genuine laughs and used that instead of a canned laugh track (if you listen closely, you can sometimes hear Damon going *A-AHHH-AHH,* because that's how he laughs). That's why the show feels live, because you have the audience's every reaction to our sketches.

There was also some aftermath to the first season. Kim Coles, who was very funny, but who was underused, was not asked back for the second season. She heard the news from her agent. Kim was managed by Sinclair, too, which made it even more difficult. As she told a newspaper reporter: "It was hard; it hurt a little bit. But I knew that it had happened for a reason. I was sad to leave a family, but it was good, too. I was not meant to be there." Kim would go on to star in *Living Single,* where she was recognized as a *star.* She's been doing great work ever since.

There was also turnover in the writers' ranks. Sandy Frank had left to work on a new sitcom called *The Fresh Prince of Bel-Air,* starring a rising rapper named Will Smith of the rap duo DJ Jazzy Jeff & The Fresh Prince. They had had a megahit with the anthem "Parents Just Don't Understand." Les Firestein, who had written for the *National Lampoon,* and Pam Veasey, a USC grad who had written for Nell Carter's sitcom *Gimme a Break!,* along with the team Adam Small and Fax Bahr, joined the show, adding to the remaining writers, which included Matt Wickline and John Bowman, who was promoted to head writer.

When Keenen introduced the second season, which began airing on September 23, 1990, he opened with a bit that was a lot like what he wanted to use on the pilot. It was about the primacy of the Wayanses on the show. Keenen called his brother Damon and sister Kim to join him onstage, and then made fun of whether success had changed them. Keenen said "they were still the same kids from the projects," while Kim flicked her hair and Damon was seemingly doper, and then Shawn (SW1) appeared with a bandage on his nose—à la Michael Jackson—all before Keenen left the stage in a custom chauffeur-driven golf cart. It was funny, but when I look back at it now, what I see is the message I missed then: It was all about the Wayans family.

Beginning in the second season, we invited hip-hop acts to appear on the show. Every hip-hop artist wanted to be on it. Rosie gets a lot of the credit for booking the dopest acts on our show. She was New York, and she was tapped into all the music coming from the streets. Many were her friends.

On our first show that season, Queen Latifah, featuring De La Soul, performed "Mama Gave Birth to the Soul Children," with Flavor Flav dancing. After her, we had everyone from Public Enemy, En Vogue, Eazy-E, Monie Love, Onyx, 3rd Bass, MC Lyte, to Arrested Development, Jodeci, Mary J. Blige, Gang Starr.

Heavy D did the show's theme song. Heavy D was the A&R director for Uptown Records, which was connected to Russell Simmons, Andre Harrell, and that whole gang.

Heavy D was born Dwight Arrington Myers in Mandeville, Jamaica, but he grew up in Mount Vernon, New York. Called Heavy D for obvious reasons—his supersized physique—he was an incredibly talented rapper, and was the first act signed to Andre Harrell's Uptown Records. In fact, it was Heavy D who convinced Harrell to hire Puffy as Harrell's intern.

Heavy D was friends with Shawn Wayans, who brought Heavy D to Keenen to perform the theme song for the second season of *In Living Color.*

Heavy D was the sole rapper of his band, Heavy D & the Boyz, which included several dancers. Tragically, one of his dancers, Troy "Trouble T. Roy" Dixon, died in July 1990 due to an accident.

So, when Heavy D performed on the third season of *In Living Color*, on May 3, 1992, he had some new dancers with him. If you look closely enough, you can pick out two of those dancers making their moves. One is Puffy, and the other young black man would later gain single-name fame as Tupac.

Heavy D & the Boyz performed an infectious version of "You Can't See What I Can See," with Flavor Flav chiming in on the chorus, and Tupac and Puffy nodding their heads, dancing, and occasionally shouting along in the background. Toward the end of the song, Tupac and Combs—who later became such bitter rivals that Combs was accused by some of having Shakur murdered—are arm in arm, bouncing up and down ecstatically.

Tupac, despite his reputation as a "gangsta'" living the "thug life," was a sweet, soft-spoken person—very shy the first time I met him.

We broke some major stars on *In Living Color*. There were those two little boys in Kris Kross (Chris Kelly and Chris Smith). Remember: "Kris Kross'll make ya jump, jump." They wore their outfits backward and the hats backward. That started a whole movement from those little boys. They were on our show and it was the debut of their album; nobody knew who they were. They went on *In Living Color* and just skyrocketed.

Paul Miller was our main director for the first two seasons. Paul had worked on *SNL* in the 1980s and was acknowledged as one of the best live-comedy directors. More important, Paul was really kind and really smart. He was really fast and really efficient. He understood people. He definitely understood me. Paul always treated me like I was an important part of what was happening.

Paul was a big, solid white guy who looked like a high school football player. He was humble, given how highly skilled he was. He put us at ease and would joke with us. He made it effortless. We had a lot of fun with him. When you were working, he relaxed you and let you do what you do. In rehearsal, he was real intense, really into the work. He understood the material. He always did his homework. He was a sharp motherfucker and really intuitive about people, too.

He picked up on how you worked. He'd remember stuff. He'd say, "Remember in rehearsal when you tried that, and you said this, and you said that. Why don't you try that there?" He'd do that while you're shooting it. Always showed us playbacks. If we didn't feel good about something, he'd say, "Well, let me show it to you real quick," and show it to us. "Well, what do you think?" You got the choice if you wanted to do it over again.

In a half-hour TV special, recorded in 2004, which looked back at *In Living Color,* Paul credited the show's success to Keenen's strong vision: "Keenen really knew what he wanted to do."

Paul recalled, "There was more freedom on *In Living Color*, more opportunity for the cast to contribute." He also pointed out that *In Living Color* was not live, like *Saturday Night Live*. It was recorded on tape in front of a live audience. That allowed them, Paul said, to be more daring and to do more production than they could have on a strictly live basis (and if you watch *SNL* now, you'll notice how many pretaped segments they include in any given show that require special effects or sets).

For example, there was a sketch in which Oprah Winfrey (who was still at the start of her talk show *Oprah* career) kept getting bigger in size. Her dress expanded like a hot-air balloon until she finally started to fly away like a balloon. It was a funny visual that would have been too compli- cated to do live.

Terri McCoy was his assistant director. Terri had worked on everything, from the TV series *Fame* to *Soul Train*. She was smart and a steady hand reining in all us crazies. She would become one of our main directors.

Tamara remained a big ball of positive energy, a cheer- leader for the writers and the actors, particularly as com- pared to Keenen. He was less demonstrative and more focused on the results. He was cold: Was it funny or not?

That second season saw the return of several characters audiences had loved. The first episode had a "Men on . . ." sketch that you can't help but smile at. David and Damon were able to get so much by the censors! They made jokes about "nuts & honey" and delivered what became an in- stant cultural meme: "Two snaps, a twist, and a kiss, can't touch this!" During the second season, "Men on . . ." reviewed their European vacation (they really, really liked Michelangelo's *David*!). In another episode, Blaine and Antoine reviewed TV shows. *Fresh Prince* was not the prince they were looking for; *Designing Women*, "Hated it!"

The "Hey Mon" sketch was back. This time, the West Indian family was staffing a hospital emergency room. During the course of the second season, the family also staffed a courtroom.

And, of course, the Homey D. Clown character was back, falling for his parole officer. In another episode that season, Homey gave lessons to Scouts visiting his Home E. Cheese restaurant.

Jim returned to Vera de Milo, doing Vera in a *Pretty Woman* parody called "Pretty Buffed Woman." This was

Jim totally committed to the character. He was crazy pushing the limits.

The "Homeboy Shopping Network" was back as well, having moved to Hollywood, with Keenen and Damon offering not only maps to the stars' homes, but blueprints and alarm codes. Whiz and Iceman attempted to sell an actual Oscar and offered advice on how to sell a faked embarrassing photo of a celebrity to the *Enquirer* or to the celebrity themselves.

For this bit, they had a cardboard cutout of Magic Johnson in a dress, which was Keenen once again burning someone he was friendly with. It was quite some burn, given that Magic Johnson's announcement that he had contracted AIDs gave rise to rumors of his having had homosexual partners. If you watch it today, it seems even less funny, given that Magic's son is happily and publicly gender fluid.

The "Snackin' Shack" sketches returned. This time, two orthodontists (David Alan Grier, James Carrey) tried to get lunch. I was still in the kitchen and making the most of a small part, ringing that order bell and deploying my spatula with verve.

It wasn't all recycling of old characters. There was plenty of strong, new material. Keenen's vision for *In Living Color* was that no one was safe. And the fact that Keenen was black meant that he felt particularly able to critique African-American leaders and celebrities. Keenen took delight in *In Living Color* taking on Jesse Jackson, Oprah, Mike Tyson, Magic Johnson, and Michael Jackson.

Keenen also seemed to take a certain delight in making fun of people who were ostensibly his friends, like Arsenio Hall. Keenen played Arsenio as an airhead suck-up talk show host. Keenen liked to make fun of Arsenio's friendship with Eddie Murphy, having the Arsenio character name-drop Eddie, or even have *I love Eddie* on the bottom of his shoes. It was funny, but Arsenio wasn't too happy about it. And as my mother would say, "Why did Keenen have to do him like that?"

One of my breakout sketches was aired in the third episode of the second season, on October 7, 1990. It was called "Spike's Joint," where I did a spot-on impression of Spike Lee.

At that time, Spike was the man. He was probably the best-known black filmmaker, perhaps the only auteur out there. Keenen made comedies. Spike made art. So it was no surprise that Keenen would take aim at Spike Lee.

In our sketch, Spike's Joint is Spike's store, where he sells everything Spike. I speak in the Spike cadence, repeating everything a dozen times, bugging the store's customers until they buy some Spike items. The running gag is that every sale comes with a free copy of *School Daze,* which no one wants. Rosie makes a great cameo, letting her Nuyorican accent fly.

It was funny. But that didn't mean that Spike liked being made fun of.

Later that year, during our show's hiatus, I was in Brooklyn and I ran into Spike in a clothing store. I was so excited to meet him. He didn't seem that happy to meet me.

"I'm Tommy Davidson," I said. "I'm a huge fan. I'm on *In Living Color.*"

"I know who you are," Spike said.

Spike told me he didn't like that Keenen had these white writers making fun of him. "Those white writers wouldn't let us talk about their leaders that way," he said.

And then, just like that, Spike walked away mad.

Another time I got to shine was when I was called upon, again, to do my Michael Jackson imitation in a parody of Jackson's "Black or White" music video. I had been doing

Michael for years in my act. So it was easy for me to do all Michael's hand motions, signature dance moves, and imitate his voice. If Michael was the "King of Pop," then I was the "King of Michael Jackson Impersonations."

Another recurring character I enjoyed performing was one half of the B.S. Brothers (the B.S. was for "black-strong"). David was Clavell and I played Howard Tibbs III, two slick hustlers trying to launch themselves in the entertainment industry with their Funky Finger Productions.

The Funky Finger men came out of this back-and-forth that David and I did just for fun when we were hanging out between sketches. Finally Keenen said to us, "Stop fucking around and get someone to write that up." We went to the writers and we did (but I got no writing credit).

The B.S. Brothers were the epitome of every jive-ass dude who hoped to climb his way to the top. It was filled with quick lines: "Look like Cicely Tyson, but sound like Peabo Bryson." Discussing a film they are pitching: "It's a cross between *Poseidon Adventure* and *Dirty Dancing*. A dancing disaster film." Loved it!

Much to everyone's surprise, the standout character from the second season would become one of *In Living Color*'s most talked-about and beloved characters. It was Jim's Fire Marshal Bill.

Fire Marshal Bill was a character that Jim had done in his act—and it came from one of the dark places in Jim's mind, of which there are a few. While demonstrating fire safety, Fire Marshal Bill would inevitably set himself on fire or cause an explosion of which he was the victim. The humor, like an *SNL* Michael O'Donoghue sketch, came from Jim's character hurting himself in increasingly outrageous and dangerous ways. There was an absurdity to it, but at the same time it was like a Three Stooges bit. People loved

The Crew (*left to right*):
My brother Michael,
my mother Barbara,
me (age 3), and
my sister Beryle,
Fort Collins, Colorado, 1966.
(Author's personal collection)

Grandpa Spence.
My best friend,
who taught me that
the Native Americans
were the good guys.
*(Author's personal
collection)*

Grandpa, Mom, and Grandma in Oregon. *(Author's personal collection)*

Larry Davidson, Fort Collins, Colorado. *(Author's personal collection)*

The Brady Bunch:
Michael, Beryle, and me.
(Author's personal collection)

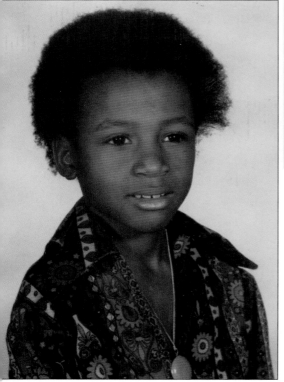

The real Black Panther
(me, age 6), Washington, D.C.
(Author's personal collection)

The sixth member of
The Jackson 5: Me
in second grade, 1971.
(Author's personal collection)

Latchkey kid, living
in Rosemary Hills.
(Author's personal collection)

Me and my mom
experience a miracle:
I graduate high school!
(Author's personal collection)

The family in Takoma Park, Maryland.
(Author's personal collection)

Me and my better half,
my brother Michael.
(Author's personal collection)

One of my mother's
greatest days,
with Jesse Jackson.
(Author's personal collection)

Mom. *(Author's personal collection)*

Michael Davidson.
Gay pride… and joy.
(Author's personal collection)

"Sammy Davis Jr. in
Mandela, the Musical":
my favorite sketch in
the *In Living Color* pilot,
which never made it on air.
(Author's personal collection)

Hammer Time.
In Living Color, first season.
*(Photo credit: In Living Color ©1990
Twentieth Century Fox Television.
All rights reserved.)*

Hey Mon, *In Living Color*.
(Author's personal collection)

Me and Jamie Foxx
in the unforgettable
Wanda Sketch on
In Living Color.
(Photo credit: Photofest, Inc.)

gas.
onal collection)

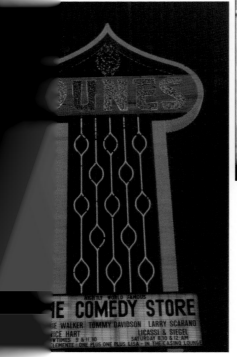

Me and Halle Berry on the set of *Strictly Business*, 1992. *(Author's personal collection)*

Me and Chris Rock in *CB4*, 1993. *(Photo credit: Photofest, Inc.)*

Jada Pinkett and me in *Woo*, 1998. *(Photo credit: Photofest, Inc.)*

Me, myself, and I (one of the few pictures where you can clearly see my Native American heritage) in 1999. *(Photo credit: Shea Bowen-Smith)*

The Magic Hour, with my mentor, Magic Johnson.

The comedy genius of Jim Carrey on display in the biggest box office success of my career,
Ace Ventura II: When Nature Calls.

The next James Bond, Double-O-Soul. *(Photo credit: Shea Bowen-Smith)*

Savion Glover and me
in Spike Lee's
underrated *Bamboozled*.
(Photo credit: Photofest, Inc)

Oscar Proud brought me
a whole new generation of fans.
(Photo credit: Photofest, Inc.)

Jessica Wilson, one of my
proudest accomplishments.
(*Author's personal collection*)

More of my greatest accomplishments
(*left to right*): Cameron Martinez
Isaiah Davidson, Jillian Davidson,
Jelani Davidson, me, and Jayden Moore.
(*Author's personal collection*)

Me and my shadow.
(*Author's personal collection*)

Amanda and me on our wedding day. *(Photo credit: Dominic Petruzzi)*

it. And Jim would return to Fire Marshal Bill throughout the show's run.

Every time Jim did, I was the costar, because no one wanted to do it. They always saved taping Jim's Fire Marshal Bill segments for last on Thursday nights, before we went to the live show. The reason for that was so Jim wouldn't have more time. Jim's a perfectionist. Jim would take four hours to shoot a sketch, but Jim taught me the value of being ultra attentive to every single detail.

Jim Carrey is not a success because he is funny. Jim Carrey is a success because his process is to troubleshoot every single aspect of what he does. And what pro doesn't do that?

I was also a fan of the characters Cephus and Reesie, which was a takeoff of Ashford & Simpson or Peaches & Herb, played by David Alan Grier and Kim Wayans. They would take any song and then soul them up in an over-the-top cocktail lounge way. In their first episode, they sang their versions of children's nursery rhymes and Saturday morning cartoon theme songs in gospel and Motown versions. In another episode, as his last wish, a prisoner gets a performance by Cephus and Reesie. In another, they plugged their Christmas album, which included a twenty-four-minute version of "Deck the Halls" and a forty-nine-minute version of "Silent Night."

With Kim Coles gone, Kim Wayans got lots more airtime. She was often called upon to play the outrageous woman blind to her own faults. In one episode, she played a wedding guest who said all the wrong things. In another, I was at the movies on a blind date with Kim, who played a woman whose insecurities made it impossible to say anything without her thinking you were saying she was fat or ugly or stupid. In the sketch, I kept trying to make her happy, until I couldn't take it anymore. And neither can anyone else in the movie theater.

Despite the comedy sketches, Kim was a serious actress, perhaps the most serious and most talented on the show (like David). Every so often, she got a chance to demonstrate that.

In "Lil' Magic's School Play," Kim played a young girl with big dreams, but not the talent to match. Kim had originally developed Lil' Magic as a monologue based on her own childhood experience. Keenen, always a spotter of talent, had her bring Lil' Magic onto *In Living Color*.

One of my favorite sketches that season was where Jim played a football coach who told the team that their end zones are pathetic. He brought in me, as a choreographer from the ballet, to train them to do dances. Then, following the script of most sports movies, suddenly they were at the big game. They scored a touchdown and then the whole team did a dance to "Disco Inferno."

That was when the Raiders were a championship team! (Hope they will be again soon!)

During the second season, we had occasional guest stars (not unlike how *SNL* lets their weekly hosts join their sketches). Perhaps the most famous was Billy Dee Williams.

When Billy Dee appeared on the set, we all went quiet. You could hear a pin drop. Because he was like the biggest star in Black World at the time. And he turned out to be just a wonderful, generous spirit to be around.

We did a takeoff of *I Love Lucy* called "I Love Laquita" in black and white, with Jim playing Ricky, Kelly playing the Ethel character. The bit was that there was a Billy Dee Williams look-alike robber; Keenen played the look-alike and Billy Dee played himself. Kim kissed Billy Dee to verify it's him. And when Keenen asked whether she was going to kiss him, Kim said, "Kiss you? That would be like kissing my own brother!" It was a very funny bit.

One of Jim's recurring sketches was "Ted Turner's Colorized Classics." It was *In Living Color*'s response to Ted Turner colorizing classics on TCM. In our sketches, we did black versions of classic films.

In this episode, we did a takeoff of *Casablanca;* which the cast called *Casablacka.* It was a black *Casablanca,* in which Billy Dee played the Humphrey Bogart role and I played the piano player as Stevie Wonder. I got to do my imitation of Stevie as he might perform "As Time Goes By."

Once again, Keenen seemed to get a kick out of portraying his friends in what I can only imagine they felt was a humiliating way. For example, Keenen opened one episode as Marsha Warfield and then did her in a milk commercial. It wasn't a particularly kind portrayal.

Keenen also had a running bit that made fun of Oprah's weight problems. In one sketch, Oprah, who was famous for her interview skills, "grills" customers at her restaurant, eventually eating a giant hero sandwich she's made. It was sort of funny but, looking back, a touch mean.

Keenen also returned to making fun of Arsenio Hall in a sketch called "The Arsenio Hall of Justice," in which Arsenio prosecuted a murder case. Arsenio (whom Keenen supplied with an exaggeratedly large butt) worked the court's attendees like an audience, and his cross-examination of the criminal (played by Jim Carrey) was done like a celebrity interview. It was complete with dropping Eddie Murphy's and Whitney Houston's names, and falling on the floor. I have to admit it was pretty funny, and relatively gentle—unless you were Arsenio and felt like you were being characterized as a fool.

Keenen and the writing staff decided to end the season

with two cliffhangers. One was "Homey Sells Out"—in which Homey played a cereal spokesman.

The other was a "Men on . . . ," in which Blaine hit his head and was suddenly straight. That was all kinds of wrong, and not funny. In fact, it took what was funny about "Men on . . ." (they saw the gay in everything) and messed with that. I can't say who or why they made those decisions, only that they did.

The last episode of the second season aired on May 12, 1991. However, Fox decided to air two episodes during our hiatus, one of sketches we had taped earlier in the year but hadn't run (August 11, 1991), and another of sketches we had (September 1, 1991).

The second season was exponentially harder than the first. We worked ourselves ragged. Keenen was a harsh taskmaster. Success did not make him more expansive and generous in allowing for other's creativity. Instead, he became more rigid and more withholding of approval. Still, we were flush with being on a successful show. After a short break, we met to start season three, with the first show to air on September 22, 1991.

Chapter 8

The Meanness

Keenen was not one to shout, scream, or lose his temper on set. He was tough—mentally and personally. He didn't have a lot of time for other people's problems, and he had a cold, mean side. Over time, he went from being collaborative to dictatorial, and, for his own reasons, Keenen liked to sow conflict. Just like the way he ran mean portrayals of his friends, he also liked to pit cast members against each other, and writers against each other. He believed that competition would yield better written and better acted sketches.

Perhaps that came from some Darwinian lesson he learned growing up in a large family. But sometimes, it just seemed as if Keenen wanted to blow it all up, to make everyone feel less secure. (In that way Keenen was Trumpesque, before Trump even was.)

Keenen wanted to stay on top, to keep control, and that was his way of making sure none of the cast members got too high on themselves.

Keenen wasn't just distant; it was also that by the third season, Keenen was spending less time on *In Living Color.*

The show was a huge success, a cultural phenomenon, and Keenen appeared to want to leverage that by creating more shows and returning to making films. The strange thing was, although he introduced every episode and occasionally appeared in sketches, he wasn't getting the attention that other cast members, such as Jim, were getting. I believe this motivated Keenen even more to try to launch new projects.

Keenen was all business, and funny was his business. As a writer, you either delivered or you were out. For cast members, you either found a way to write funny sketches or you were relegated to minor parts. Keenen didn't care how late you worked, how burned out you were. You either did the job or you were out.

That worked some of the time. However, it was difficult to maintain positive feelings about a show where you felt unappreciated, not on solid ground, or where the hours were impossible. It used to be that people didn't want to leave the set or offices; they wanted to hang. Now they couldn't leave.

The meanness spread throughout the show: The writers' room had a wall where they put up bad sketches and made fun of them. Cast members who were not writers, or whose last name wasn't Wayans, found it increasingly hard to get their own sketches on the air.

For all those reasons, by the third season, *In Living Color* was not the happy, creative place it had been that first season. Keenen and Tamara also announced several changes for the third season.

Our director Paul Miller left the show. Terri McCoy, who was very talented in her own right, would end up taking over for him. There was turnover among the writers again. Bowman left to create *Martin*. Fred Graver and

Michael Anthony Snowden joined the staff. Firestein was now head writer, along with Pam Veasey.

There was a new dancer from New York, a Puerto Rican woman, named Jennifer Lopez. Ever heard of her? I had met her when she came by the set of *Strictly Business*. I may be wrong, but I think Keenen brought her to set. Were they dating?

Rosie had spotted her at auditions for the second season, but for whatever reason, Carla Garrido was chosen. Now Jennifer was replacing Carla. The other girls weren't so happy about the newcomer—and not so welcoming. They had been working twelve-hour days under Rosie's strict discipline and they felt Jennifer would have to earn her spot alongside them.

There were new cast members as well. Steve Park was a Korean American who played a deli owner in Spike's *Do the Right Thing*. He joined the cast for the third season (Park met Kelly Coffield on *In Living Color*, and many years later they would reconnect and marry). I was glad that our cast was becoming more diverse. Asian Americans represented a sizeable portion of the American TV-watching audience, yet there were no Asian-American comedians on TV.

Keenen made Shawn a cast member, which didn't do a lot to lessen the feeling that this was the Wayans comedy half hour. That was tough for Shawn, who felt he had earned the spot.

And there was another new "featured" cast member, Jamie Foxx. Jamie had been performing stand-up for some time at the Comedy Act, and he was known to be quite a good singer.

Here's how I found out about Jamie. I was on-set for rehearsal, waiting in the break room, and Keenen walked in like he was getting something out of the refrigerator (which I'd never seen him do before and I assume was planned on his part). So he said, "Hey, buddy!" And then as he was leaving the room, he turned and told me that he had hired Jamie. As Keenen was quick to point out, Jamie could do everything I could do. It was a not-so-subtle message from Keenen to up my game. Or that I was on the way out. I could have reacted in a number of ways, but what I said was:

"It's your show, man. You can do whatever you want, am I right?"

And that's how we left it. That night, I called my aunt and told her about the conversation with Keenen. "Did that make you feel insecure?" she asked, adding before I could answer, "Jamie Foxx can't be you, and you don't need to be Jamie. Being you has got to be good enough."

One of Jamie's breakout sketches that first season was playing Wanda, the character he'd done in his audition. Wanda was a frighteningly ugly woman (and truth be told, Jamie in drag made for one ugly woman). What made Wanda funny was that she was superconfident and assumed she was the most beautiful woman in the world.

In that first Wanda sketch, which aired on the third season's first episode, the scene opened with me lying facedown on a massage table. Wanda started describing herself as looking like Vanna White, and the joke was that I am falling for her. Imagine that in one of the first sketches of the new season, Keenen wouldn't even let my face be shown. What message was I being sent? But I gave back as good as I got: Consider that I was able to make this scene work, even though I was lying facedown! That wasn't easy. Jamie was so over-the-top the scene worked great.

I'll tell you, though, when we filmed that sketch in front of the audience, Jamie did something that was not in the script. He yanked hard at my underwear, trying to rip them off to leave me butt-naked. He yanked at that thing as hard as he could.

Remember I was facedown, so no one could see my re-action. That was a good thing. Because my first reaction was to sit up and bust him in his mouth, saying, "What the fuck, motherfucka!"

Then it dawned on me. This could be comedy gold. This could be like Lucy in the candy factory. And it was. I don't think it was Jamie's intention to do anything other than get a cheap laugh at my expense. How it played out in the end just made me want to hug Jamie for making me the focus of a comedy sketch that viewers would replay millions of times, to this day.

Once again, Keenen and the writers returned to characters they had created in the prior seasons.

Keenen found new ways to make fun of Arsenio. This time, he had Arsenio interview juvenile delinquents. The idea was funny, but the execution—well, it was just more needless teasing. It was just more negative energy the show didn't need.

The "Hey Mon" family (the Hedleys) were back, running a restaurant, but in this episode they met the Korean grocer, played by Steve Park. He and his family have opened their store next door to the Hedleys' restaurant. Park was revisiting the same character he played in *Do the Right Thing*. The joke here was that the Korean Americans might be even more hardworking than immigrants from the West Indies. It was broad stereotype vs. broad stereotype in a way that you probably couldn't do today. Watching it now, the sketch seems out-of-date, if not somewhat racist, but that was where *In Living Color* lived—at the edge of what was acceptable and sometimes past that line.

Handi-Man was back with "The Adventures of Handi Boy," a look at Handi-Man's boyhood and how he received his powers. As I mentioned, Damon was deeply invested in his disabled hero, Handi-Man. What the writers did here was basically rip off Superman and give Handi-Man the same backstory: parents from a different world, and him discovering his powers as a child from a hologram of his parents talking to him. It was more clever than funny, but the tension in the character was Damon's elevating a character that did not look super. And let's not forget that Blade and Spawn aside, it would take more than twenty-seven years before there really was a black superhero on the big screen.

Damon also had another handicapped hero, the Head Detective, who was just a head, large hands, and no body. A lot of the humor came from him being tossed or kicked across the room, or from situations where he was being manipulated as part of a remote-controlled body. It was absurdist humor, but Damon played him as a smart detective and the audience took to him.

I got to do the Funky Finger men again with David Alan Grier. This time, our scheme was to promote cheap vacations. David and I had great chemistry in those sketches. And audiences really responded. Everyone knows a hustler.

One of my favorite sketches that season was "Adopt a Child Star." In it, Kelly Coffield did her Sally Struthers impression, with Kelly/Sally making an appeal for the Adopt a TV Child Foundation. Call 1-555-Has-Been, "Do It Now." She is pitch-perfect talking straight to the camera, asking to help these former child stars.

Kelly had been doing her Samantha Kinison impression on *In Living Color,* and one of the highlights of the third season was her doing it again. But this time, in "The Kini-sons at Home," she was joined in the scene with Sam Kinison himself. This was like when Tina Fey did Sarah Palin when Palin guest-starred on *SNL*. It was wild, funny, and it totally worked.

I knew Sam from the Comedy Store. He was a mean lit-tle dynamo who exuded great personal power—and anger. But he was always saying, "That was outstanding, man." My set was astounding. His set was astounding. And al-though he played an out-of-control, on-the-edge character, when Sam came to do *In Living Color,* he was a profes-sional in every way.

After I made the film *Strictly Business,* Keenen seemed to take the potential success of my movie career person-ally. That was not a good thing. During the third season, Keenen acted like I had already left the show.

I may have had my own three-phase plan with Sinclair Jones, but let's be clear: Keenen had his own plans. *In Living Color* was Keenen's show, and it was also the Wayans Full Employment Act. Keenen was like "the Godfather" of the Wayans family, and he wanted to steer all of them to success. Keenen would find great success with the *Scary Movie* fran-chise, but that was years off. Right now, he was frustrated.

That may be why when the buzz on *Strictly Business* was such that it looked like it was going to be a hit, Keenen didn't seem to want to share in the good news. You would have to ask him what was really going on in his head. All I can say is that once I did *Strictly Business,* Keenen lost all interest in me. My ideas made it to the stage less, and I was cast in fewer sketches, and I was rele-gated to being a background or supporting character.

When the premiere of *Strictly Business* was set for New York at the end of October, a big gala with all of New

York's hippest party people and entertainment executives, I started to hear from my reps that Keenen didn't want me to go. Worse yet, some of my friends warned that if I did go, I could possibly be fired for breaking my contract.

Let me say this: I wanted to go. I really, really wanted to go. It was my moment in the sun. I couldn't believe that Keenen, whom I loved, Keenen, who had given me a career, would ever fire me for going to the premiere of my first movie. So I confronted Keenen and asked to go to the premiere in New York.

Keenen said that he understood that I wanted to be at the premiere. He said he wanted me to be able to go. He just asked that I call him on Thursday at five to make sure that no issue had come up for that week's show that would prevent me from going.

Five o'clock, Thursday night, rolled around. I called. The phone rang, and rang, and rang. No assistant, no receptionist, no voice mail. No answering machine. I called again and again and again. No answer.

I didn't know what to do. I didn't know what Keenen was thinking. Did he forget I was going to call, or was it something more sinister? It's a dangerous thing when you don't have all the facts. Back then, my mind favored the paranoid.

My lawyers were saying that if I went, Keenen could have cause to fire me. But I so wanted to go. I felt this was the start of the next phase of my career and I had to seize the moment.

I asked Sinclair Jones what I should do.

"Fuck Keenen," Sinclair said. "You're going to the premiere of your movie. You were Tommy Davidson before you met Keenen, and you'll be Tommy Davidson after you leave the show. Let's get on with your career."

So I went to the premiere.

* * *

The *Strictly Business* premiere was held October 28, 1991, at New York's Ziegfeld Theatre, on West Fifty-fourth Street between Sixth and Seventh Avenues. The premiere was a benefit for the Black Filmmaker Foundation and the United Negro College Fund. Warner Brothers, which wasn't really prepared to market this movie to African Americans, still knew how to host a premiere.

It was everything I had dreamed a movie premiere could be. There were klieg lights lighting up the sky. There was a red carpet and a satin velvet rope holding back the crowds of onlookers eager to see celebrities. It was Halle Berry and Joseph C. Phillips and Sam Jackson.

It was black tie and I wore a tuxedo, with some hip black satin neck band rather than a bow tie. Halle wore a simple but gorgeous dress that was short with a plunging scoop neckline. That dress told the world what we all knew: Halle was one of the most beautiful women on the planet.

There was plenty of press from every major media outlet. But I'll tell you what meant a lot to me. Photographer Malcolm Pinckney, who would go on to be one of the preeminent photographers of New York City's parks, took a shot of a radiant, smiling Halle, flanked by me on Halle's right and Joseph on her left, both kissing her on the cheek. That photo ended up in the December 2, 1991, issue of *Jet*. In Black World, that was better than appearing in *Time* magazine.

The audience loved the film, laughed at all the right places, and there was a giant ovation of applause at the end of it. Nelson George was there with his mother and some nieces. When the screening ended, one of the first people I saw was Keenen's dad, who couldn't have been nicer. He was a reminder that Keenen comes from a great family.

The premiere was all I had imagined, all I had dreamed of for so many years (even if Halle continued to be angry with me; even if I feared Keenen was plotting against me). It was, simply, my greatest achievement to date.

However, by the next day, I had lost the ability to enjoy the moment. I was making myself crazy with worry about Keenen.

Thank God for my agent, Michael Gruber at William Morris, who did what a great agent does: He talked me off the ledge. He explained to me that, in fact, Keenen couldn't fire me because my contract for *In Living Color* was not with Keenen. It was with Fox, the network that owned the show. The only person who could fire me, Gruber said, was Peter Chernin, who was then the head of the Fox Network.

To this day, I don't know if what he told me was true or not. But that calmed me down a lot. I went back to L.A. and back to work on *In Living Color*.

Keenen didn't say anything against me. However, because I had gone against Keenen, and put my own interests ahead of his and ahead of the show's, it was never the same. Right or wrong, I felt Keenen did not support my success. That was emotionally devastating to me, and it could have been career-threatening. This was the start of a really tough, tough time for me.

In saying this, I don't mean to take anything away from Keenen and his massive talents as a creator, producer, writer, director, and comedian. I have tremendous respect for Keenen. If it hadn't been for Keenen's genius, kindness, and brotherhood over the years, I would not have had the career I had. And his family has embraced me as one of their own. But, at that time, in those moments, I was suffering.

From then on, my airtime got less and less. And my paycheck didn't get any bigger. It turned out that T'Keyah and I were the lowest-paid members of the cast by a wide margin.

Jamie wasn't used that much in the first half of season three. He was only a "featured" player, not a full cast member. After I attended my premiere, Jamie, who I fully admit was very talented, suddenly got a lot more play. As the season progressed, you saw more of Jamie and less of me.

Jamie was competitive, and his brand of humor was being mercilessly mean. When Jamie found out he could score points with Keenen or the writers by making fun of me, he was nonstop, 24/7, on my case. Keenen seemed to love Jamie teasing me. He never once told him to lay off.

If I had a scene with Jamie and he was chewing up the scenery at my expense, I would look to Keenen to cut, but he never would. Jamie was the new flavor of the month. Teacher's pet. He was all that.

I hadn't given up completely. I still went into the writers' room with ideas for characters or sketches. But they, too, had turned mean. They took some of my ideas and put them up on the wall of bad-sketch ideas, and then Jamie and the writers would bring up my idea relentlessly as the worst.

There's nothing you can do if the executive producer's like, "This is what we're doing," and every time you come with an idea, he says, "No."

When I finally got a sketch that I knew was really great, they just mocked me, and made me feel ashamed for even trying. Everybody kept saying, "Here goes Tommy again with that sketch." I would say, "I'm doing like everybody else." They made me into the laughingstock of the show. (Ironically, during the fifth season, when my ideas finally got traction from the writers, they were among the most popular of the series.)

At the time, being mocked that way really hurt. I had been a partner in the show since before there was even a pilot. My ideas and characters had been loved by the first season's writers. Those writers, such as Sandy Frank and Matt Wickline, knew that if they gave me a character, I would explode it. I would make it ten times better on-screen than it was on paper. And, then, suddenly my ideas sucked. Really?

I get it that making fun of someone else sometimes makes you feel better about yourself. But we were all cast members, and I could still recall that first season when the cast felt excited every day. We used to be the Beatles in *A Hard Day's Night*. It was difficult to admit that we were now the Beatles of *Let It Be:* angry, petty, and dispirited.

Did it bother me? Of course. Did I know how to deal with it? Not really. Here's what I knew: I wasn't going to let Keenen or anyone else grind me down. I was not a quitter.

I am not saying all this to lay blame for my problems on Keenen. My problems were all my doing. I'm hoping to explain what made me vulnerable to making the bad choices I made. Like an arson detective, I'm trying to find the igniting incident, the catalyst, the accelerant that blew up my problems. In the end, it was not feeling appreciated, and being isolated—all of which threw gasoline on the fire of my core abandonment issues. The bad atmosphere didn't help. And this business does strange things to the human mind. Especially mine.

Today, with hindsight, I might look at the situation and wonder why I stayed. Was it my history of taking abuse and my lifetime about being silent about it, pretending that it didn't matter? Was that what made me put up with

Keenen's abuse? Did I not feel myself worthy of being treated better? That may be true. As anyone who worked with me then would tell you: I had my own demons and my own way of dealing with them (like everyone else does, including Keenen).

But back then, I was determined to make the best of the situation. And I did: I started to spend more time with the crew, more time with the directors, more time in the producing booth. I was learning every aspect of making a show.

The more episodes you see of these, the less you see of me in these sketches. Any skit I was in, I made the most of. And I learned a new skill: being the straight man.

The cartoonist Bob Thaves once wrote: "Ginger Rogers did everything [Astaire] did . . . backwards and in high heels." I learned the art of supporting my fellow actors. Suddenly I saw in a new light what Stan Laurel did for Oliver Hardy, what Gracie Allen did for George Burns, and what George Bush did for Jon Stewart.

The Academy of Motion Picture Arts and Sciences used to give Oscars for the category "Best Supporting Actor." Most people think of this as actors performing in a lesser or smaller part. But, in fact, it's for the art of supporting the main actor, of making their leading performance all the stronger.

For this reason, whenever Jim Carrey did his Fire Marshal Bill character, he wanted me in the scene. Damon wanted me in his Homey D. Clown scenes. And whenever Jamie did his Wanda character, he wanted me in the scene. Jamie being mean to me didn't stop me from supporting him in every scene we had together. But off-camera, and when the show wasn't shooting, we didn't hang out, we didn't socialize, we barely talked.

* * *

In spite of everything that was going on, or because of everything that was going on with me, I was surprised when one day after a rehearsal, Keenen circled the cast because he had an announcement to make.

"We're doing a live special," Keenen said. It was going to be a live episode of *In Living Color* to air opposite the halftime of Super Bowl XXVI in January 1992. And then he added, "Tommy's hosting." Keenen knew that I could rock live, that was my strength. Still, I was surprised.

The Super Bowl has always been one of the most popular shows on television (if not *the* most popular). In the first years of the Super Bowl, the halftime show was mostly marching bands, until they introduced a performance by Up with People, a positive upbeat troupe performing wholesome positive programming. It was safe and not very exciting. The Up with People singers were going to perform again at Super Bowl XXVI in January 1992. The official NFL halftime show was called "Winter Magic," which consisted of a skating performance from Brian Boitano and Dorothy Hamill, and a song by Gloria Estefan, all with a Winter Olympics theme.

The Super Bowl was on CBS. Fox decided to counterprogram the Super Bowl halftime show by broadcasting a live episode of *In Living Color,* "The *In Living Color* Super Halftime Party" (also referred to as Season 3, Episode 16).

For us, this was a tremendous opportunity. Doritos agreed to sponsor our halftime show. We had no idea how many people would turn the TV channels to us at halftime. But one thing I knew for certain: We were going to be funnier and more interesting than Up with People. No offense to them; just telling the truth!

The show opened with the "Homeboy Shopping Network, Super Edition," with Keenen and Damon selling tickets to the game, uniforms to play in the game, player cards—or rather players' credit cards—and then jewelry, jewelry, jewelry!

Jim did a wild performance as Fire Marshal Bill. The sketch was set in a sports bar during the Super Bowl, where everything that could go wrong did. It ended with a clip of the *Hindenburg* exploding as if it were the Goodyear Blimp.

In another sketch, I played Sugar Ray Leonard interviewing some of the celebrities there, such as Blair Underwood and Pauly Shore, asking each of them if they were enjoying the nachos, if they were enjoying the guacamole, and enjoying the festivities. And then I threw it over to a special "Men on . . ." sketch.

Fox had arranged for a slight tape delay so they could bleep out any problem material. The problem was that David and Damon knew how to get their material by the censors.

The *Men on Football* TV show opened with Antoine and Blaine talking about Dick Butkus, which pleased them to no end. Then they went on to how much they loved Cowboys and Buffalo Bills playing with the Oilers and the Packers. They milked the double entendres for all they could.

And then at some point, David (the Antoine character) said, "Joe Namath is married. Hello?"

To which, Damon (Blaine) replied, "Well, so is Richard Gere, but you should have seen that gerbil in a wedding dress."

Which no one could believe Damon said . . . and that *no one bleeped*!

And then, before anyone could recover, Damon threw in this one: "You know why Carl Lewis runs so fast? You can run, but you can't hide from your true self, Miss Lewis."

Carl Lewis was an Olympic legend, so to take on his private self was just *bad*!!! *Crazy!*

And there was more crazy stuff: In one of the sketches, I played a sportscaster interviewing the coach. Just to show you how long ago it was, and how much different a time it was, the sportscaster I was imitating was O.J. Simpson! Can you believe that?

The coach was played by Jamie Foxx (still listed as a "featured player" rather than part of the "cast") in a hallway, while Jim photobombs the interview (about twenty years before photobombing became a thing). "Background Guy: Super Bowl Interview" was a very funny bit.

And it wouldn't be *In Living Color* without our Fly Girls and a musical guest. In this case, Color Me Badd, a multicultural boy band out of Oklahoma City, who sang their hit "I Wanna Sex You Up."

And then, before we knew it, it was over.

The live episode was directed by Terri McCoy and choreographed by Rosie. And, yes, hosted by me. They would never take that away!

We didn't know it then, but when I look back, the Super Bowl might have been the high point for *In Living Color*. We had some 20 to 25 million viewers switch to Fox from CBS's presentation of the game. No one has done anything like that since.

Enough people had switched channels that CBS decided that the next year they needed to up their halftime game in a major way. Which they did: They got Michael Jackson to perform. Ever since, it's been one high-profile musical act after another for Super Bowl halftime viewing—and no channel changing!

That was a high point, no doubt. The rest of the season was a grind. Still, there were a few standout sketches and some that meant a lot to me.

Given that my Sammy Davis Jr. sketch in the pilot was killed, I never imagined I would ever get to do him on *In*

Living Color. However, I finally got to do my Sammy Davis Jr. impression in a remake of *Ghost* where Sammy is the spirit advising them.

On the show's last episode of the season, I did a bit where I'm the *Wide World of Sports* reporter interviewing Super Clyde—a Super Dave Osborne–type daredevil played by David, only this time he's braving doing stand-up at the Apollo.

I also got to do the last sketch of the season, which was a parody of *The Dating Game,* where the bachelorette in question was Jamie Foxx's Wanda. In "Ugly Woman: Dating Game," Shawn was bachelor number one, I was bachelor number two, and David was bachelor number three. Jim Carrey was the "obligatory host," as he described himself. If you watched this scene today, you see I played well off Jamie, and there was a good give-and-take chemistry in the scene. But what I'll always cherish was how Jim and I got to go crazy after I was selected as Wanda's date.

I can't describe how I did it—or what exactly Jim did—but somehow I leapt into Jim's arms and he spun me all around his body. It was one of those you-can't-quite-believe-your-eyes moments. It was straight-on insane physical comedy and we brought it. I think all of Jim's and my frustrations exploded in that scene. Man, were we laughing afterward!

The end of the season was notable for Keenen using it to say good-bye to Damon, who, Keenen said, was off to his "superstar movie career." It bears pointing out that he had said no such good-byes to Kim Coles or other employees who left the show. Once again, being a Wayans was more important. Keenen was the closest to emotional he'd ever really been on the air.

It had been a tough season for many reasons. The show had a lot of problems. Jennifer Lopez was one. Jennifer was very ambitious. She didn't see herself as just a dancer. She was always lobbying the writers to get on a sketch or to perform. The writers didn't take her talent seriously (and, boy, were they wrong). Rosie was a hard-ass, and she and Jennifer didn't get along. Rosie wasn't great at handling any opposition, so it just added to the tense atmosphere on the set.

And Jim wasn't happy, either. Jim, T'Keyah, and I were like the outcasts of the show. There were social occasions, times when a party was set up to take place on the set, and we were not invited. I kid you not. Chips and snacks would be set out, drinks would be set up, and we'd be walking out with our backpacks, saying, "What's going on here?"

Other times, we would hear that *Entertainment Tonight* or *TV Guide* was coming to the set. We would get all spruced up, only to find out it was just the Wayanses who were being interviewed or photographed. And we would only find out as we sat on the sidelines.

We became our own little unit, the three of us. But it got under our skin.

Jim also didn't like that, like me, his ideas were constantly being rejected by Keenen and the other producers. Jim was also increasingly becoming a supporting player to the Wayans family members. By the third season, Jim believed that he knew what worked and what he could do, and he had proved it on many occasions. Jim was a fan favorite and he had earned the right to get his sketches on the air. But Keenen wasn't interested in a democracy. The more Jim protested, the more he shut him down.

Keenen didn't react well to non-Wayanses becoming stars, a lesson I had learned as well. And Jim didn't take Keenen's attitude well. Unlike me, Jim was not a "go-along, get-along" guy.

At the next table read, with Keenen in his usual spot at

the head of the table, Jim was supposed to read his part in a sketch. So Jim stood, turned around, and read his part as if it was coming out of his ass. And it was not just that Jim was being a ventriloquist and throwing his voice, he was also moving his butt muscles so it really looked like he was talking.

The room went quiet. As I mentioned, Keenen was always in control of himself; he rarely showed anger or any emotion at all. Keenen pushed back his chair and stood. He stayed there for a second. Everyone in the room thought he was going to deck Jim, or that Jim was going to lunge at him. Eric Gold, who was both Keenen and Jim's manager, was in the room. He stood up between the two.

But Keenen just walked out of the room.

No one had ever stood up to Keenen. And no one had ever dissed Keenen in so crude a way.

Jim understood that he had to apologize, and that if he didn't, he would be fired.

Jim was courageous as hell. He went into Keenen's office. Smoke was pouring out of Keenen's ears.

"Do you like your job?" Keenen asked Jim.

"I love this job," Jim said. "I'm sorry. I was angry."

And after that, they both moved on. But, once again, the show was never the same.

By the way, there was one *In Living Color* sketch that you won't find on DVD. It ran once and never again, on May 5, 1990. "Bolt 45" was a takeoff of a Colt 45 Malt Liquor ad. What may have seemed like a funny idea—Bolt 45 knocked its drinker out—turned out to imply that it could be used as a date rape drug. Not funny. Which is why it never aired again. And this was years before Bill Cosby.

Speaking of Bill Cosby, Jamie did a killer imitation of Bill Cosby. He did an impression in "The Cosby Condom" sketch (December 15, 1991), which sounds a lot different today. But the voice, the mannerisms, I give it to him. Jamie killed it.

When I look back at the third season, I feel just like Bruce Lee when he said, "If I were the man with the money, I wouldn't give me the money to make the movie because I'm Chinese." Cast members who had been there since the beginning, such as Jim, T'Keyah, and me, were not allowed to shine the way we were in the first season. So I followed Bruce Lee's advice, which was, he said, to "express myself in a human way." He said, "No matter what you do, if you express yourself genuinely from your human center, things work out." That was the philosophy I tried to follow. My mantra became "Just be all your Bruce Lee."

I did Kung-Fu, Wu-Su for about two years as a kid and then I got into amateur boxing as a teen and competed nationally. As a matter of fact, I ran into the guy that I fought for the Potomac Valley finals, which was for the Olympics. There are all these different regions. It was Golden Gloves and AAU. I won the Golden Gloves for my region and then went for the championship, and I lost to a guy named Vincent Pettway in the last round, because I got too winded. And the reason I was too winded was because for the weeks before the match, I was hanging out with the guys in my neighborhood, smoking weed, and I just kind of stopped doing my jogging and training.

Ironically, I ran into my boxing coach years later, after *In Living Color,* in a mall in St. Louis, of all places. That was where he was from and I was in St. Louis to play a club. I had run into the mall with some friends to get a new shirt. His name was Napoleon Jasper.

I see him there and I was like: "Napoleon?" He was

like, "Wow, Tommy! Wow, nice to see you." Just as humble as always. He turned to the people that I'm with and said, "Tommy was one of the most gifted boxers we had on the team and he never lost. He lost just one time." He paused and then added, "But the thing that hurt Tommy's boxing career was that he was always joking. He was really, really gifted, but he wanted to joke the whole time, on the bus to the fights all the way, all day at the gym. I used to say, if he ever concentrated, he's either gonna be two things. He's either gonna be a damn comedian or a boxer. I'm just so glad he became one."

A similar thing happened when I went to visit the veterans in the actual hospital where I had worked in Washington, D.C. Many of them had lost limbs. I went to visit one of the veterans I had met before. He had stepped on a mine and had one leg amputated; the other leg was still functional. But when I came back, they wouldn't let me upstairs to see him. So, instead, I decided to go down to the kitchen where I used to work.

Downstairs, there were two old black ladies who came out and said they remembered me. They just started crying and hugging me. One of them turned to me and said, "You were such a wonderful kid." She said, "I remember when I first started working here and I heard this voice from the back singing and I walked back there. There was this little boy putting boxes away, singing his ass off, and I said to him, 'Man, you got to do something with that one day.'" She started crying and said, "I'm so glad you did."

One more story, about these strange and meaningful encounters. I'm at an Oscar party that I'm hosting and I'm standing out, waiting for my car. I'm talking to the guy next to me and he said, "I'm a boxer from D.C."

I said, "I boxed in that system when I was a kid." We found out we were the same age. I went, "Wait a second, what's your name?"

He answered, "Vincent Pettway."

I said, "We fought each other for the . . ."

He said, "I know. I never thought I'd see you again . . . but I've been watching you all these years."

That's some shit, isn't it?

Chapter 9

Alien Abduction

Although I appeared in several sketches in season four, those were actually sketches shot earlier, which Keenen had banked and then decided to air that season. I was not on-set and did not film any new sketches for the whole fourth season.

What happened to me? I was kidnapped by aliens.

Extraterrestrials took over my body and brain and took possession of me for most of that year. They did experiments on me and subjected me to all sorts of questions and examinations. It was all alien to me. They took my blood and urine. They forced me to talk about myself endlessly. I was held in a series of cells, each more uncomfortable than the last. They asked me to pledge allegiance to their leader. This went on for the better part of the year. And if asked to tell you about it in great detail, there is very little I remember.

And that's as true as the fact that I spent the whole year trying to get sober, going from rehab to rehab, getting clean and relapsing. In the end, I went from someone who could no longer function to someone who could. But despite what I believed at the time, I was still fooling both myself and others. The aliens still had a hold on me.

In truth, I barely made it to the end of the third season. I had shit going on at work, and shit going on at home. I didn't have the tools to fight for myself. Instead, I retreated and developed a drug problem.

Here's the thing about drugs and alcohol. At first, they help to quiet your social anxiety. For a moment there, everything's funny and you feel like you're the life of the party. However, if you are already feeling alienated and paranoid at work, and people are making fun of you, then addiction will make you exponentially more withdrawn and disconnected. Increasingly I had a hard time showing up. I became very uninspired. And no one seemed to miss me.

Not being on *In Living Color* was, in many ways, a giant relief for me. Being blackballed and made fun of was very stressful. It wasn't fun and it was killing my spirit.

Now, all I can say about that is that a person who was left as a baby in a trash pile does *not* take well to being treated like garbage. Add substance abuse to that, and I was digging myself an early grave.

But back then, I wasn't thinking about all that. All I was thinking about was surviving.

I had first dabbled in cocaine while making *Strictly Business* in New York. I was out at a club one night, the China Club on the Upper West Side. Down in the darkness there, I had my first drink in eight years—and I won't lie, it felt pretty good. Then I ran into someone I knew from D.C. It was one of the guys who sold cocaine back in the day. He asked if I wanted some. I said yes. And that's how it started.

When the movie finished and I went back to L.A., I assumed I would never use again. I was wrong. I was hooked.

Whether it was psychological, or physical, or both, doesn't really matter. I did not stop.

Everyone on *In Living Color* knew I had a problem. I thought I was managing. I thought I was hiding it from them. But everyone knew.

I was doing all the not-good things you do when you have a drug problem: Your "problem" becomes your full-time priority and everything else comes second. I went from the hardest working, most professional person to someone who just wasn't showing up.

Eventually I lost my mind and I knew I needed help. I was no longer leading a life and I needed to get the skills to return among the living.

Keenen was a stand-up person. When I told him that I needed to get help, he said, "You do what you got to do. You take care of yourself. I love you." That was Keenen all the way: He was all about solving problems. He wasn't emotional. *In Living Color* was family to Keenen, and he extended his brand of tough love to me when I needed to get help. At the time I was just trying to survive but today I am grateful to Keenen for letting me even acknowledge that I needed help.

When I left the show, T'Keyah said something that meant a lot to me. She said, "You know at least one thing for sure. You are getting an opportunity most people don't—to understand in your own lifetime what your limits are."

I went from treatment place to treatment place, twenty-eight days at a time: in Arizona, in Indiana, in California. I was moving imperfectly, and with great difficulty, to recovery. It was a hard lesson to learn that I was not in control. I kept trying to take my recovery into my hands. I believed that only I could make myself stop. The exact opposite was true. I could only change when I took the ad-

vice of the people around me and followed a path laid out
for me and just concentrated totally on what the people
around me were telling me. But I wasn't ready to realize
that yet.

I probably went to eight different places a total of
eleven times. People will say to me that if you went that
often, it must not have worked. And I tell them: "No, it
worked, because if I didn't go back all those times, I'd be
dead." So that's how it worked. Not all at once, but over
time.

People say that to spend that much time there, there
must have been a lot that was wrong with me. There was.
And none of it had to do with *In Living Color* or
Hollywood. It had to do with me.

I had a lot of shame around not being an upstanding
person. From high school on, I was always about being
upstanding. I worked the jobs; I took the buses; I supported my girlfriend; I fathered the children and supported
them, too. My whole life, including all my Bruce Lee philosophy, was about improving myself and becoming this
superperson: the hardest working star in show business.

During my time among the aliens, the most important
thing I learned is the simplest: I was human. A human
being. I lied; I hurt people; I let people down—like all humans do.

My perception of that ideal person I wanted to be was
taking things too far. I had charted too perfect a path for
myself, where there was no room for mistakes.

It wasn't an ego thing. It was more like a survival thing.
If I can be perfect, then I can right all the wrongs I see.
And everything about that premise is wrong.

I had to learn that I was not in control of everything, and I
had to pass the mantle of all powerful, all seeing, all knowing, to a higher power. Me, I was just human. I wasn't Doro-

thy in the magic kingdom of Oz; I was Dorothy in Kansas, taking shelter with her family from a tornado.

I had to learn to forgive myself and accept myself as the imperfect human being that I am, before I could stand a chance of being back among society. I had to be willing to say that just being Tommy Davidson was enough.

When I was ready to return to *In Living Color*, for the fifth season, I discovered that for all intents and purposes, I had neither been fired nor quit. Turns out that what I had done was take a leave of absence to deal with a medical problem. That was a right my contract allowed me to do (this is why having good agents and lawyers can be so important). I was still under contract for another year of *In Living Color*.

The fourth season had new cast members. One was another Wayans, Marlon. The other was Alexandra "Ali" Wentworth, who had been part of the Groundlings, an L.A. improv group. The fourth season also introduced D.C. comic David Edwards, whom I used to see in the clubs. He was in a few sketches, but wasn't moved up to "recurring featured performer" until the fifth season. Edwards often brought his best friend to the set, another D.C. comic, Dave Chappelle. I used to see Chappelle perform when we were both starting out.

In order to boost falling ratings during the fourth season, they had guest stars, like James Brown, Mario Van Peebles, and Rodney Dangerfield, of all people.

However, before I rejoined the cast for the fifth season, some major shit had gone down: Keenen had fought with Fox and had left the show. No small event.

As I heard it, the fight had to with syndication. *In Living Color* had racked up some seventy episodes by which point it made sense to start discussions about syndicating the series. In the traditional network TV model, syndication was where people got rich. They made a good living while the show was on the air, but it was in syndication that people made fortunes.

The pilot for *In Living Color* had been produced by HBO, but the series was produced by Twentieth Television, a division of the same Rupert Murdoch–owned company that owned the Fox Network, where the program aired.

The story goes that when Fox decided to fill holes in their programming with reruns of *In Living Color*, Keenen felt Fox was trying to hurt the syndication value of his show. And when it appeared that those syndication rights would be sold to FX, yet another Murdoch division, Keenen saw self-dealing and double-dealing practices to lessen what would end up in his pocket.

The final straw for Keenen, as reported in the *Los Angeles Times*, came when he and Fox tangled over the repackaging of show highlights. Keenen felt Fox had no right to air "best of" shows, feeling the reruns would harm the future value of the show in syndication.

Now, whether this was accurate, or was just a negotiating position, I have no idea. All I know is that things quickly devolved. There was even a story about Keenen hiding a master tape of a program above one of the ceiling tiles in the *In Living Color* offices and holding it for ransom.

Whatever was going on, the net result was that by the end of the fourth season, Keenen had left the show. Tamara followed him out the door. So did Marlon. Shawn and Kim were still under contract and were expected to remain. But the truth is, you don't want to have cast members on a sketch comedy show who don't want to be there, so Kim and Shawn were released from their contracts and left the show.

Veasey, Fields, and Firestein, who had been appointed producers when the season began, were elevated to executive producers. They were happy to take control of the show.

Jim was happy, too. He'd had enough of fighting with Keenen.

After the fourth season, from May to July 1993, Jim had spent the hiatus filming *Ace Ventura: Pet Detective*. The movie was an outlandish idea. Many big-name talents had turned down the original script before it made its way into Jim's hands. To his credit, Jim felt there was something there that he could work with, that would allow Jim to be Jim in ways that would make the film work. So, in typical Jim fashion, he obsessed. Jim spent hours between his sketches reworking the script, trying out bits for scenes. And once they were shooting the movie no detail was too small for Jim to improve. Once, he spent four hours just to get the hairpiece right for his character. And he was not wrong: On the poster, what you notice is Jim's hair.

The movie wouldn't be released until February 1994, a year in which Jim would also appear in *The Mask* and *Dumb and Dumber*. Finally he would be recognized for his comedy genius. But for the time being, Jim was happy to remain at *In Living Color*.

It had not been *In Living Color*'s strongest season. And with Keenen gone, no one would have been surprised if Fox decided to cancel the show. But Fox didn't really have a worthy replacement, and they only profited by having more episodes in their library. So Fox picked up *In Living Color* for a fifth season.

I had a show to go back to!

Chapter 10

My Favorite Season

Leading up to the fifth season of *In Living Color,* the producers and casting agents scoured the comedy clubs for new talent. Once again, they considered Dave Chappelle, but decided he was not ready yet for the show. They also considered John Leguizamo, who wanted to do the show, but he was talked out of it by his agents.

As Leguizamo explained to a reporter from *Details:* "You know your representation talks in your ear, and the whole thing gasses up your head. They're like, 'You're blowing up, John! You've got to have your own show, John.'"

In the end, *In Living Color* signed Jay Leggett, Carol Rosenthal, and Anne-Marie Johnson. Chris Rock agreed to appear as a "special guest star."

Jay came to the show from Chicago, where he'd studied under the legendary improv teacher Del Close. Jay was a big guy and he brought a big personality to the show. He was from Tomahawk, in Wisconsin (no joke). Leggett was a hunting enthusiast and would die of a heart attack in 2013, following a hunting outing in Tomahawk.

Carol had worked with former *In Living Color* writer Buddy Sheffield on a Fox sitcom called *The Edge.* When that show was canceled, she was offered a spot on *In Living Color.* She understood comedy and was great in a scene.

Johnson was a great talent. She appeared with me in *Strictly Business,* had been in Robert Townsend's *Hollywood Shuffle,* and Keenen's *I'm Gonna Git You Sucka.* Along with others, I recommended her to the show and was glad she became a cast member.

Marc Wilmore, who'd been a writer on the show, but had appeared in some sketches, was made a cast member for the new season. Larry Wilmore, his brother, was added as a writer. Larry Wilmore would go on to fame on *The Daily Show* and his own late-night program, *The Nightly Show.* Nick Bakay and Colin Quinn also joined the writing staff. Nick, who'd been a writer and contributing editor for the *National Lampoon,* had appeared as an actor on several shows (and would continue to do so while pursuing a successful comedy writing career). Nick even provided the voice for Salem the cat on *Sabrina the Teenage Witch.* Colin Quinn would become known on *Saturday Night Live* and for his one-man shows.

There were, of course, cast members from the fourth season whom I had not worked with, such as Ali Wentworth. Ali was great because not only could she play to type (WASP girl), but she was even better when she was cast against her type.

When all was said and done, it was the largest cast we'd ever had. This was good, in that we had a deep bench and the writers had a lot of targets they could write for. At the same time, it made production unwieldy and increased the competition and difficulty in getting on air.

There were other changes as well. Jennifer Lopez had left the show. Rosie had left, too. Rosie's talent was greater than choreographer alone. She had shown what an amazing actress she was in *White Men Can't Jump*. Rosie left the show in capable hands. Her second in command, Arthur Rainer, took over.

Paul Miller was back as a director and as producer. I was happy about that. Paul was my guy. He knew what I could do and I trusted him to bring out the best in me.

Although *In Living Color* was Keenen's show in almost every respect, *not* having Keenen or his siblings there had some positive benefits. You know how some people are "yes men." Well, Keenen had become a "*no* man." There was no pitch you could come up with that Keenen didn't believe he'd heard before, and had already said "no" to. Now anything could be pitched (even if it had been before). Everyone had a chance. Every voice was heard. Cast members were psyched to contribute. This allowed the show to be fresh, inventive, and fun—in particular for the veterans like me and T'Keyah.

It goes without saying that once we were no longer the Wayanses' show, it literally opened up a lot of acting opportunities. It was also fair to say that Pam Veasey, Les Firestein, and the other writers had been there long enough, were professional enough, and had written for the show for enough seasons, that they no longer needed Keenen's direction, management, and criticism.

All of which made for a much happier set. Aside from the first season, the fifth season was my favorite year of *In Living Color*. We gave it everything we had, and had a great time doing it. Plus I had shed a lot of my shame and anxiety; I felt a lot freer. I was happier and that made me more fun to be around.

From that fifth season, there were many standout sketches: "*Seinfeld* in the 'Hood" was a brilliant response to the fact that the New York–set *Seinfeld* had no black people in it. Jim knew Jerry from the clubs from back in the day and his imitation of Jerry is a spot-on exaggeration of the way Jerry could go on about anything ("What is the deal with the way black guys shake hands?"). Jay Leggett does a funny George Costanza, while Carol did a Kramer that hit home. Jamie and I played street guys who end up mugging Jerry and George and taking over Jerry's stand-up slot at show's end. It was funny and pointed because Fox had moved the show to Thursdays up against *Seinfeld*—and it was a battle we were not destined to win.

In "Ike Turner Strikes Back," David did a credible Ike impersonation and made as much fun as he could of a guy who beat women and saw nothing wrong in that. That's one of those sketches that might have been funny at the time, but today it makes one cringe.

"What if Andy Rooney Were Black?" or "A Few Minutes with Randy Rooney" was full of the piss and vinegar that Andy Rooney doled out weekly. This time, though, it was directed at Rooney and privileged majority-white culture. My favorite line: "What would the White Plague be? Tennis elbow?" I love that line!

Perhaps the most famous moment of the fifth season happened off-screen. It had to do with a sketch I was in with Jamie Foxx involving our characters Ace and Main Man, who were doing security at a Tupac concert.

When Tupac had first appeared on the show, he'd done so as a dancer. He was a kid. A sweet kid. In less than two short years, he had become a major star, a celebrity in his own right.

Everyone was excited about Tupac appearing on the show. The setup for his scene was that Jamie and I were playing security guards at a Tupac concert, guarding the stage entrance to his show, and trying to make the most of what little power we had, while people were trying to get backstage—particularly attractive women. Then Tupac himself showed up.

At first, we don't believe he's Tupac. We hassle him. But, finally, we let him in.

Jamie played someone who was a player in his own mind, and I channeled some of the street people I used to do in my act, with a stutter and that kind-of-mumbled ghetto talk.

Tupac appeared on the set and was, again, gentle and shy. We did our scene. As usual, I was able to support Jamie, but also got big laughs. It all went very well. I got to talk to Tupac. He was a great, beautiful, humble human being.

It was only much later, when a lawsuit against Tupac was filed, that I learned a completely different story of what happened that day.

As was the custom with guest appearances, Fox had sent a limo to bring Tupac and his entourage to the set.

I didn't see any of this occur, but what I heard was that when the director told us to take a break after filming our scene, Tupac and his entourage went out to the parking lot to hang out in the limo Fox had sent them. They lit up and the driver asked Tupac to stop smoking marijuana and put out all of their joints.

According to accounts, words were exchanged, and the driver said something about Tupac having no respect for rules because he had no father and no role models. At that point, Tupac's entourage beat the driver senseless. Whether Tupac was still present when this happened, or had already left the limo and was on the *In Living Color* set, is a matter of some dispute.

The bottom line was that I certainly didn't know what had gone down in the parking lot and Tupac's appearance on *In Living Color* was a big success and was another notch in his evolving acting career. A few months later, he would start shooting what would be one of his major roles as a troubled basketball player in *Above the Rim*, directed by Jeff Pollack, who would, a few years later, have a great impact on my own acting career.

One of the great joys of the fifth season was how beautiful it was to have Chris Rock around. Chris doesn't play the "I'm more important than you" game. Despite having been on *SNL* as a cast member, Chris wasn't really an actor or an improv guy at that point. We talked about that and I shared with him what I'd learned from the first seasons of *In Living Color*.

Chris was funny as hell. He had his own characters and one of them, Cheap Pete, became a regular feature that season. The thing about Cheap Pete was, simply, that he never wanted to pay for shit—and if he did, he didn't want to pay full price.

Cheap Pete was the kind of guy who goes, "How much for a doughnut?" When the store owner answers, twenty cents, Cheap Pete counters, "How about for eleven cents you give me a bite of it?" That was his shtick.

I was either the guy giving Chris the doughnut, or the guy in the store, or I was near him all the time. I worked through those sketches with him and had a lot of fun with Chris.

During season five, Jim was allowed to fly. He brought back Fire Marshal Bill and Vera, but he also did some crazy shit. As part of his stable of comic characters, Jim had Background Guy (he'd launched him on our live Super Bowl episode) and his Overly Confident Gay Man. He also had some crazy new characters, like Umbilical Barry, a college-age kid who has never cut the cord between him and his mother (played by Carol).

With Keenen no longer there, Jamie lost the glow of being the Sun King's favorite. He wanted to do his own ideas. Some were good. But some were not: Jamie had this bit he was desperate to get on the show where he played a monkey. He didn't see it as racist—just as a way-out character. I'm glad it never got on. Today I'm sure Jamie is happy, too.

"Unpoetic Justice" was a takeoff—or rather a take-down—of John Singleton's Janet Jackson movie, *Poetic Justice*. The joke in the sketch was that the bad poetry and random thoughts, which were the internal monologue of the Janet Jackson–like character, made fun of Janet as some-one who was wealthy and playing "ghetto." No disrespect to John Singleton who was a beautiful human being, Buddy Sheffield wrote "Unpoetic Justice," but I came up with some of the material for that sketch and was given a writing credit. That was something that would not have happened in the Keenen era.

In "Carl 'The Tooth' Williams's Paternity Suit," I played an attorney suing a boxer (Jamie Foxx) in court. Again, I got to run my mouth a lot and drive the sketch in which Jamie showboated as the prizefighter.

Sweet Tooth Jones was a character that I was allowed to fully develop. I had been waiting for years to get the op-portunity. In "The Hollywood School of Self-Defense," viewers see that his whole knowledge of karate was com-pletely taken from 1970s blaxploitation movies. All his moves were fake movie moves. He talked scenes from movies, but eventually his students, who actually knew karate, kicked his ass.

I did several sketches as Sweet Tooth Jones. In one, "Sweet Tooth Jones: Sexual Harassment Seminar," I'm the instructor at an office that deals with sexual harassment and self-defense. This aired back on April 28, 1994, and we're just dealing with this now!

In some ways, it's like a black version of Jim's sketch from the first season, "Bad Karate Class." At some point in each sketch, I take off my karate uniform, my *gi*. When one student complains, "You don't know karate!" I an-swer, "I never said I did. I am a fight choreographer from

Hollywood." It was fun because I got to dance, sing, do my karate moves, and just be silly. And I was the star of the sketch. I didn't need to do my best in the background. I was up front—and outtasight!

I can't tell you how wonderful it was for me to be able to go into the writers' room and pitch an idea and have them want to work on it with me. To collaborate, to create, to have one's ideas respected, to be heard—I don't know what's better than that.

We were having a good time. But our ratings were down. I don't believe it was because the quality of the shows had lessened. I think our declining ratings were a reflection of being up against *Seinfeld*.

To improve the ratings, the showrunners turned to having more guest stars, such as Marsha Warfield, Gary Coleman, Barry Bonds, Johnny Gill, Fred "Rerun" Berry, Biz Markie, and Luther Vandross.

That last season, there was one sketch ("Prison Cable Network: *Lights Out with the Angel*") that was an issue for me. It had a solid premise: I played Angel, the host of a show on the Prison Cable Network. That was a workable idea. However, I guess because it was the Prison Cable Network, the writers had filled the sketch with what I felt were homophobic, gay-bashing jokes. I had a problem with that, in no small part because my brother, Michael, had raised my consciousness about gay issues.

Michael was my big brother. Three years older than me. He was smarter than me, and he was sharper than me. We had been the best of friends and we would always tell each other so. Since we were little kids, we would ask each other the question "Who's my best friend?" He'd say, "Tommy. Who's my best friend?" I would answer, "Michael."

Michael was the emotional glue in our family. Michael sent cards to us. He made sure all the birthdays were right.

Our mother facilitated them. She'd make a pumpkin cake. She'd make her fruit salad every time on Thanksgiving. She cooked all the food, but Michael was the guy who made sure everybody enjoyed themselves. His capacity for having a good time, and not caring what others thought, sometimes embarrassed me when I was young. For example, we went to a Parliament Funkadelic concert, and I got this white boy in a top hat, holding a cane with a snow globe on top, just going crazy.

Michael was the one who would create the circus in the backyard. He'd do the bicycle rallies. He'd scare the livin' shit out of us at Halloween. Michael was the dude, and it was an eye-opener, because he was my big brother.

But in other ways, he struggled, too. He never went to college. He dropped out of high school at sixteen, got his GED, and then hitchhiked across the country. He ended up spending some time in Colorado with our father, Larry.

Eventually he returned to D.C. and got an apartment. He even managed me at the start of my career, driving me around to gigs. We lived together briefly, but when he couldn't pay his share of the rent, I was mean to him. I kicked him out. And although he had not come out yet, and I didn't know he was gay, I used to call him "faggot."

Even then, I knew that was wrong. My mom didn't allow that kind of talk in the house. Racial or ethnic slurs were not just a no-no, they were a *not ever*. I did so, anyhow, when we lived together and I was filled with remorse about doing so for years and years.

Fast-forward to many years later: Michael was living in Seattle. He had come out as gay by then. We had patched things up. I knew he loved me, and I loved him. He had become a community activist for gay rights.

Michael was a member of ACT UP. In 1991, when the University of Washington Medical Center decided that HIV-infected medical staff could no longer perform surgery without the patient's consent, Michael went to their luncheon board meeting, jumped up on the table, and ordered them to rescind the policy. Instead, they moved the luncheon.

His AIDS activism wasn't limited to Seattle. He was among those who went to Washington and before Congress; he contributed to the AIDS quilt, which was first displayed on the National Mall. He lobbied Congress to devote funds to AIDS treatment and finding a cure. He was one of the guys that did that.

Michael's lover was among the first to die of AIDS. Soon after, Michael discovered he was HIV positive. At the time, there weren't the lifesaving, or life-extending, drugs for HIV infection that exist today. He got sick. And he got sicker.

My mom and sister went out to be with him. They were carrying him to the bathtub, washing him. Helping him shit and pee. Doing all that.

My mom called me to say, "He's got about, maybe, a week left. You might want to come up and stay here."

I went up to Seattle and spent a few days with Michael. It was very tough to see him like that. But I went and I said what I had to say to him. Told him I loved him. I apologized again for calling him "faggot" as a kid, and he apologized about not paying his part of the rent and running up my credit card with his charges. And we laughed about it.

He said things that were very important to me: "I want you to know that people are going to react to you differently, and with hostility, and negativity, because of your specific background. They're going to pick up something's really different about you and be afraid. Just know that it's not because they don't like you, it's because you're strange to them." And that was something that stuck with me. That kept me going when people would treat me like shit for no reason. That was our last conversation.

He hung in there. I then had to go to a stand-up gig. I was ready to cancel it, but the promoter said, "Well, if you cancel it, I'm going to go on the radio and say you're back on drugs."

My mom said, "Go. Michael would want you to be performing."

I went, and that night, while I was onstage, Michael died.

After Michael died, I went back up to Seattle. My father, Larry, was there. We'd been estranged for several years—in part because I felt like he favored the other kids over me. That was mostly in my head. But when Michael died, that just drew us close together. We became the best of friends and remain so, to this day.

Michael had schooled me in understanding HIV and AIDS. In 1991, when Magic Johnson announced that he had tested positive for HIV, I called him, because I knew what Michael had gone through. Michael was still alive then and I told Magic, "I'm here with my brother. Anything you need, or anyone you need to speak to, Michael knows them. If there's anything I can ever do for you, you let me know. I know this is hard, but I know that you're going to be okay."

He said, "Thank you, man. Thank you for that call."

I still feel tremendous guilt that I was not there when Michael passed. As for the prison sketch, Michael was still alive when we filmed it. I called him to ask him for advice. He said, "Just make it funny." Michael was very understanding. But I wince whenever I even think of that sketch.

I'm going to tell one more story about Michael and my mother. For this, I am going to jump ahead to 2006. My mother had just passed of an incredibly rare form of cancer. We had held the funeral and I was driving back to my hotel. It was nighttime, and as I was driving through Silver Spring, Maryland, I decided to go by the house where we grew up.

I walked up to the house that held so many memories. I opened the door and walked into the entryway. The layout of the house was such that facing the entryway was a staircase that led to the second floor, where the family's bedrooms were.

I was going to walk into the living room when something caught my eye at the top of the stairs. It was like a little flash of light. I looked closer and was about to walk up the stairs, when I saw it.

It was my brother, Michael. He stood there, looking much as he did before he got sick, with a half-smile on his face that I knew so well.

I was frozen in my tracks. He started down the stairs and got halfway and stopped. And there behind him, I saw my mother. She was standing there, too, right behind him, and she put her hand on his shoulder.

I didn't know what to think, but I felt something—a warmness—a feeling that I can only describe as well-being. I understood that my mother and Michael were together now, and they were all right. They would be watching over me until that day when I would be together with them again.

In one of the last shows of *In Living Color,* T'Keyah, who was one of the last original cast members standing—who, like me, had suffered the slights of not being a Wayans—and I got to do a final sketch as tweens Deronda and Pookie having a play party.

We worked in some burns on that sketch. So, for example, when I said to Pookie, "Let's play 'positive black role models on television,' " she put her head inside a cardboard TV and said, "Hello, everybody!" That's when I pulled a blanket over her and said, "Sorry, you're canceled." That was right on target and reflected the producers' concerns that we would not be renewed for a sixth season.

If you want irony, the last performance that season was a musical performance from a long-forgotten rap trio with a name that, in hindsight, feels like an inside joke: To Be Continued. The group performed their song "One on One." As they took the stage, they shouted out: "Ain't no party like an *In Living Color* party, 'cause an *In Living Color* party don't stop!"

But the party was over. About a minute into their performance, the credits began to roll, and then the screen faded to black. No one got to thank the cast, the crew, and the audience. No one got to say good-bye.

We didn't know if *In Living Color* would be renewed for another season. It stood a chance, just because Fox didn't have much else better to air. But, one day, we just got the word. Nope. Canceled. That was all she wrote.

I didn't mind. I was prepared for cancellation. I felt ready to take on new opportunities. Chaos is part of every entertainment career. If I wanted stability, I'd still be a cook in Maryland.

The end of *In Living Color* wasn't really the end of an era. In fact, *In Living Color* can be more correctly described as the beginning of an era—an era of multiracial and African-American comedy on American network television. When *In Living Color* debuted, the only other shows on air at the time that had significant diversity or that starred African Americans were *The Cosby Show* and *A Different World*.

Since *In Living Color* had first aired, you had *The Fresh Prince of Bel-Air*, where Sandy Frank was a writer, *The Sinbad Show*, where Michael Petok was a producer (as well as on countless comedy specials and *The Bernie Mac Show*),

Martin, which John Bowman cocreated, and which Matt Wickline and Sandy Frank executive-produced. Kim Coles starred in *Living Single. Sister, Sister* was cocreated by Kim Bass, and *Hangin' with Mr. Cooper* starred Mark Curry, who took over for me warming up the studio audience on *In Living Color.* That is more than a legacy. It is an avalanche of talent.

Chapter 11

The Show Goes On

When *In Living Color* ended, I was one of the youngest cast members, and my career was just taking off. During the years of *In Living Color*, I'd become established enough, and had enough fans and supporters who knew what I could do, that I continually got work on television and in film. For example, in 1992, during our third season, I was hired to be part of a live version of the TV show *Roc* on Fox.

Roc was played by Charles S. Dutton, a great theater actor who had recruited a lot of talented actors to work with him. In this episode, "The Hand That Rocs the Cradle," I played a homeless guy whose wife (Debbi Morgan, Dutton's real-life wife) gave birth to a stillborn baby. I gave a dramatic performance, and everyone was crying.

Let's pause here for a second. When the writers wrote this episode, they didn't know anything about my personal history. But imagine that here I was, a person who had been abandoned as a child, discovered in a garbage pile, and now I was being called upon to play a homeless person with a baby born in an alley—and that baby dies.

And if that wasn't heavy enough, consider this. As a teenager, Dutton had been a boxer nicknamed "Roc," who killed a man and served seven years for manslaughter. Now he was an accomplished actor with his own series on network TV, and I was hired as an actor to perform with him. A convict and an abandoned child, and we both were succeeding in Hollywood. If that's not the American dream—if that's not some shit—I don't know what is.

But there's more to the story. As I mentioned, the show was done live. Dutton had some guests there to watch. Among them was Spike Lee.

After the performance, I went up to Spike and told him that when we'd last met in Brooklyn, he'd treated me wrong. "Hey, man. You hurt my feelings, man."

Spike said, "No, man, I didn't mean that, man." We became friends that day.

And that led to my being in *Bamboozled* later.

In 1992, I did an uncredited cameo in *CB4,* a movie Chris Rock cowrote and which Tamra Davis directed. I played a VJ (video jockey, like from the MTV days) who's playing Chris Rock's music video, and the whole thing is a sendup of the rap scene—early on.

One of my favorite guest spots on a sitcom, and one that people continue to come up to me about, is when I played Varnel Hill on *Martin.* "Hollywood Swinging" was a two-part episode that aired in November 1993, during *In Living Color*'s fifth, and final, season.

First of all, Martin Lawrence and I had been friends from the start of our careers back in D.C. Second, Matt Wickline and Sandy Frank, two of my favorite writers from *In Living Color,* wrote for *Martin.* John Bowman, who was also from *In Living Color,* was one of the creators. Finally, Sinclair and I had parted ways and Martin and I now had the same manager at the time, the legendary Sandy Gallin. (If you don't know who he is, look him up! The man was a legend and Dolly Parton's partner.)

Varnel was actually written by Matt. He had the character already punched out and he knew I could play it. Varnel was an over-the-top, Arsenio Hall–type character, full of himself, who appeared on Martin's local radio show. Martin was interviewing Varnel on the radio, trying to find out how successful Varnel was.

Martin asked my character what kind of car he drove, and I answered, "I don't have a car." That made Martin happy. Then Varnel said, "I don't have a car. I have a limousine, a Mercedes limousine." And so it went, every time Martin asked Varnel about anything, he topped him by telling Martin how wealthy and successful he was. And the moment Martin showed up in L.A., Varnel ignored Martin.

It's strange how art imitates life. At that time, Martin was experiencing a lot of success and it was putting him through a lot of changes. His personality was totally different from the guy I had known back in the day. The Martin I knew was a really humble, great guy. Now, with his own show, he'd become something of a tyrant. It bothered me how he behaved toward the cast and crew.

I actually pulled him aside and said, "Man, when did you start talking to people like this?"

At the time, Martin said to me, "You don't understand, man, this is TV."

I was like, "I've done television, man. Come on, man. Done TV before you."

He was used to giving orders, but I showed him how we could add a little improv to the scene, which he wasn't used to doing. But he took it in and let me do my thing.

And if you watch that episode now, you can tell where Martin and I were tearing it up—and I was trying to keep it together because he was slaying me. Turned out to be two of the best episodes.

I hope Martin understood that all I wanted for him was the best. I think he did, because we've remained good friends. We're closer now than we were then. He recently did me a big favor: appearing as the closer at a comedy benefit at the Laugh Factory for the Sarcoma-Oma Foundation charity.

Let me share a rather amazing moment I experienced because of Varnel.

There was one night when I was sitting alone in a hotel room, feeling bad. I was in Amsterdam, which is a whole city organized around the proposition that no one has to feel bad. Ever. But, for whatever reason, that night, I couldn't go to sleep. It was three in the morning, and then four, and I was wide-awake. My mind was filled with negative thoughts. I kept telling myself that I needed to get back on a TV series. No one knew who I was; no one cared about the work I'd done, and the work I could do. I was beating myself up, thinking there was something wrong with me. It was a dark moment.

I turned on the TV in the room and started scrolling through the channels. And there, on the TV in my hotel room in Amsterdam, was *Martin*. And me as Varnel. And it made me feel better. I told myself: "You don't have any problems, man. You're sitting in Amsterdam, and they're playing your thing on TV."

True story. And I learned a lesson: Do your work; don't complain; don't play the head games where you compare yourself to anyone else. Because if you let it, that shit just turns around on you.

*   *   *

About a year after *In Living Color* ended, Jim Carrey called and said, "I got a part for you, man. I know you're going to love this thing." It was for *Ace Ventura: When Nature Calls* (the sequel to the original). I didn't have to audition or anything. They just gave me the part.

They were filming in San Antonio. I guess I didn't realize Jim was becoming such a big star until I got to the set and saw Jim's newfound clout in person.

After I finished my scene, there was a scene where this African warrior buries Jim in the dirt up to his neck. The burying was going too slow for Jim's taste. So Jim halted the take and said, "Get me a bulldozer." I thought he was kidding. But in fifteen minutes, a bulldozer showed up, came right over the hill. Like he had asked the waiter for a glass of water. I mean, who can summon a bulldozer on demand?

Working with Jim on *Ace Ventura: When Nature Calls* was both a professional and a personal highlight. Never have I had so much fun on a movie that was so successful (to date *Ace Ventura: When Nature Calls* has earned more than $200 million in worldwide box office receipts).

A few words about the best job that any actor can have: voice work. You would not believe the number of great actors and talented comedians whose real source of income is voice work: doing voices for commercials or animated films or TV series, or even being the background voice in a scene. If you have the knack for doing so, it is wonderful work and it can pay well.

Early in my career, I did a lot of cartoon work. I did a lot of voices for *The Simpsons*. I would just go in and do different characters for them, for, like, thirty-five bucks. A lot of anonymous character work. And that work saved my life. There was six or seven hundred dollars coming in, in a week, when I really needed that money to live. It made a real difference.

I also had a lot of fun doing voice work. So, for example, on *Ren & Stimpy*, I played a Sammy Davis Jr.–type praying mantis. For me, anytime I got to do Sammy, that was a win-win.

Beyond that, I appeared in many movies that I enjoyed thoroughly, even if they weren't big box-office smashes.

For example, one film that I very much enjoyed, which not many people ever saw, was the comedy *Plump Fiction*. Yup, that's right. It was a takeoff of *Pulp Fiction* and all those Quentin Tarantino–type hard-edged neo-noir films. I played Sam Jackson's part, which was a kick for me.

Bob Koherr, who wrote and directed it, was a wonderful director and a really innovative guy. He'd started his career as an actor and *Plump Fiction* was his directorial debut. He's gone on to a successful career as a TV sitcom director, having directed multiple episodes of everything from *The Drew Carey Show, George Lopez, Wizards of Waverly Place*, and *Hannah Montana* for Disney, as well as *Anger Management, Jessie,* and, most recently, *Bunk'd*.

On *Plump Fiction*, I got to work with the very funny Sandra Bernhard and Julie Brown, and such pros as Dan Castellaneta (the voice of Homer Simpson) and Colleen Camp.

Although not a lot of people saw *Plump Fiction*, the right people saw me in it, even before it was released theatrically. I will always be grateful, because it's what got me considered to star in the '90s comedy classic *Booty Call*.

Booty Call is also notable because it was the first major movie role for Jamie Foxx. Foxx had small roles in the romantic comedy *The Truth About Cats & Dogs* and a Sam

Jackson movie, *The Great White Hype*, in which Damon Wayans also appeared.

Jamie was very excited to star in *Booty Call* playing the supporting role of Bunz, the straight man to the lead role of Rushon, which was to be played by Bill Bellamy. That is, until I auditioned for the role.

The movie was directed by Jeff Pollack, a talent manager, who had been one of the creators, writers, and producers of *The Fresh Prince of Bel-Air.* Jeff had written the screenplay for and directed *Above the Rim*, a well-received film that provided Tupac Shakur with one of his first major film roles.

My agent had convinced Pollack to see me, even though he had his mind set on Bill Bellamy. I was keenly interested in landing the role, because although it was a raunchy comedy, it would be my first part where I was a romantic interest.

I went in to audition. I was so in the moment that, looking back, I don't remember what I said or what I did. It's one of those things that happens sometimes when I do stand-up: I turn on, the magic happens, and I can't tell you afterward what went down. This was like that. It was just magic. I felt good in the room. But they sent me home and told me I didn't get the part. They decided to go with Bill Bellamy.

I don't know what went wrong, but they couldn't make a deal with Bill. So, when I least expected it, I got a call: I got the part. I didn't need to audition again. I was in!

The plot of *Booty Call* is pretty simple. The IMDB website lists it simply as: *Two friends who have gone too long without sex set out to get some.*

Among the producers were John Morrissey and Lawrence Turman. Turman had been a producer on *The Graduate*. So we had some steady hands who knew what they were doing.

Cut forward to the first day on the set with Jamie. It

was clear that he didn't understand the concept of "supporting actor" or even saw himself in that role. He was determined to steal every scene he could. That led to a fair amount of tension on the set.

One day, while we were waiting for Jeff to set up a shot that took place on a basketball court, Jamie challenged me to a game, saying, "Let's play to eleven, and I'm going to shut you out, eleven to zero."

First, a little background: Jamie Foxx was born Eric Marlon Bishop. He, too, was adopted. He grew up in Terrell, Texas, which was a racially segregated community. He grew up very much in the Black Baptist Church, where he sang and played piano. He was a high school football star and also played basketball. So, no question, he had game. But his game was football. Basketball was just high school ball. I played one-on-one on the public courts in D.C. That was a whole different game and I was determined to take Jamie to school on that.

Jamie Foxx is a stage name he took in L.A. Recently, when he appeared on *Colbert,* Jamie explained that when he first got to L.A., he was trying to get stand-up slots onstage. Jamie had noticed that when he put down his name, Eric Bishop, he was just one of many, many male comics trying to get a slot. So he started writing down names that could pass for male or female, in the hopes that they would call a female-sounding name sooner. One night, at the Santa Monica Improv (a branch of Budd Friedman's Improv club that used to exist at Fourth at Santa Monica, and from which they used to shoot the TV show *Evening at the Improv*), he signed up as "Jamie Foxx." They called his name, and he went onstage and killed. Standing ovation. And that was it. He was Jamie Foxx.

So, back to our one-on-one. He threw me the ball—

boom, boom, layup, 1–0. Jamie started talking trash, but that was not helping his game. 2–0, 3–0, 4–0.

A crowd had gathered. I can't deny that I was enjoying making Jamie eat crow. And losing was not bringing out the best in Jamie.

At 9–0, I announced that I was going to shut him out and shut him up. I went up for a layup and Jamie charged me, putting his football talents to use by tackling me.

If I had hit my head on the hardtop concrete, that would have been the end of me. I was lucky that my street smarts conditioned me to ball up when going down. I was ready to give Jamie some street-fighting lessons, too—but the crew pulled us off each other and held me back.

I ain't proud of it, but I was defending my house. Since fifteen, I'm 20–0 in my fights. As a little kid, I got whupped plenty of times. But since I turned fifteen, that changed. I grew up with my shit. I've got my rage. I can street-fight. I learned how to box. I did martial arts. So if there was a fight, I was going to win it, whatever it took. But I was lucky I was held back, because beating on Jamie would have been on me.

So that was Jamie. Talented, no doubt. When I saw *Ray,* Jamie gave an amazing performance. He has driven his career to amazing places—not only winning an Oscar, but also winning a Grammy and being a featured performer on recordings by Jay-Z, Kanye, and Diddy.

However, at the time, I found him lacking as a human being. His behavior on *In Living Color* and *Booty Call* hurt my feelings. We never talked about it. But back then, he was not that reachable emotionally. He had his issues and I had mine. Maybe he's a better person now. I would like to believe he is.

When I was not on camera, my job was to learn as much as I could. I spent a lot of time with the movie's director, Jeff Pollack. He walked me through a lot of what he was doing, the decisions he made. I always made it a point to be the director's best friend on the set. If he needed me to work with one of the actors or say something that he felt he couldn't say directly, I would do so from my perspective as a fellow actor.

On *Booty Call,* I got to work with Tamala Jones and Vivica A. Fox. Tamala Jones had mostly appeared in music videos, TV programs, and had a small role in *How to Make an American Quilt,* but she was a natural. She had that special quality that when you saw her on the screen she seemed real. She has gone on to a long career in TV, having a major role for several years on the hit TV show *Castle.*

Vivica Fox was probably the most experienced actor on the set. Born in South Bend, Indiana, Fox had come west to attend college and soon after started appearing on daytime soap operas, such as a leading role on *Generations* and on *The Young and the Restless.* She'd appeared on sitcoms like *Fresh Prince* and *Martin.* On film, she played Will Smith's girlfriend in *Independence Day,* and had been part of the crew in F. Gary Gray's *Set It Off,* with Jada Pinkett (not yet married to Will) and Queen Latifah.

As a director, Jeff was meticulous. He was a perfectionist, really observant, really skilled. Jeff often turned to me when he was having problems with the other actors not getting along. He was very collaborative that way. That made me feel good and also improved my skills.

A good example was when Bernie Mac came in for a scene in *Booty Call.*

Bernie had been given a scene, but he couldn't quite seem to get into the role. Jeff told me that if Bernie couldn't get going, he was going to have to cut the scene. I said, "Give me a minute to talk to him." I had an instinct I could talk to him. So I said to Bernie, "I get it. This scene just isn't in your language. So tell me how you would say it." And we went to my trailer and Bernie went through his scenes and I wrote them up in his language. And then we brought that to Jeff, and after that, Bernie was flawless.

Because of that process, and because Jeff trusted me, *Booty Call* made me a better actor. However, I wanted to show that I could do more than balls-out comedy. I wanted to show that I could carry a romantic comedy as a lead. And I got just that chance in my next major motion picture, a movie called *Woo*.

Woo was a very important role for me. The competition for the role was strong. Many actors who were already romantic leads auditioned, including Morris Chestnut and Isaiah Washington. These were hot guys. And here I am at the audition, too, this comedian.

Daisy von Scherler Mayer (Daisy V. S. Mayer) was the director. There were not a lot of women directing, and even fewer women directing comedy, so this was very much a film that was breaking barriers. She had directed the cult independent film *Party Girl,* which launched Parker Posey's career.

I'm sure Daisy was one of the major reasons Jada Pinkett wanted to do the film, and she trusted Daisy to steer her in a romantic comedy as the lead character, Woo.

Woo was a rom-com about a very sophisticated woman named Woo and what we would today call a "nerd," a guy who was the shy one in a posse of players. During the course of one night, they discover they are destined for each other. In my audition, I was asked to read with Jada.

Jada had grown up in Baltimore, where she attended a performing-arts high school. She had found early success in Hollywood, appearing as a freshman in the TV series *A Different World* and then getting significant roles in *The*

Nutty Professor and in Keenen's *A Low Down Dirty Shame*.
Keenen had been an important person in Jada's career and I
was nervous that he might have soured her on me.

That proved not to be a concern. Jada was a down-to-
earth, straight-ahead, no-bullshit person. I auditioned doing
some scenes with her and she was great. I got the part. And
I believe Jada approved me for the role as well.

Once shooting began, Jada and I became fast friends
and got close. We were like kissing cousins. I had come to
the movie prepared. I had memorized the whole script. I
knew my part, her part. I could run lines with her and we
talked about the script.

We also talked about our lives. Jada told me that she
had met Tupac in high school, and she spoke about their
close friendship over the years. She was now dating Will
Smith, who was solid in all the ways Tupac never could be,
but Tupac had died a violent death only six days before
shooting on *Woo* began. Tupac's death affected her deeply.
She cried telling me about him.

I had met Will Smith in 1987 in a recording studio when
he was still a music artist. I thought he was solid. We were
always cool.

I told her about my family and my own difficult up-
bringing. She was a sympathetic listener. A true friend.

We were several weeks into shooting, when my mother
called me on the set.

I was like, "Hey, Mom. What's up?"

My mother just blurted out: "I found your birth mother!"

At the time, my mom, Barbara, was working for Housing
and Urban Development (HUD) and had access to all these
databases. She got it in her head to search out my birth
mother.

She started with Greenville, which is where she had last

seen her—some thirty-odd years before. As fate would have it, there was only one Tommie Gene Reed residing in Greenville.

Now you might think that this is where my mother shares this information and leaves it up to me to decide what I want to do. That is one possibility.

My mother was more like a dog with a bone. Once she got it into her head that she was going to find my birth mother, she wasn't going to stop there. Apparently, it was something that had been weighing on her for many years without mentioning it to me. She just picked up the phone and dialed her number.

"She sounds good," my mother said. "She wants to meet you. Would you be willing to meet her?"

At the time, I just couldn't believe my mother had gone ahead and called her without asking me.

"Didn't you think of calling me before you did that?" was all I could say.

It was hard to explain what I was feeling. I had such confused feelings about my birth mother and so many questions about why she abandoned me. I wasn't sure whether seeing my birth mom was in some way being disloyal to the woman who had raised me and was my mom. I was feeling all kinds of hurt and anger. It brought up all kinds of emotions I wasn't ready to deal with.

Looking back, and after thinking about this for years, I now understand that my mom always saw herself as my guardian, that she was caring for me while my mother couldn't. She never wanted to replace my mother. And now that I was doing so well—starring in a movie—and she was doing well—working at HUD—my mom felt it was time to reach out to my birth mother. Hearing that she was doing well, she wanted to reconnect us.

But I couldn't handle it. We were in the middle of rehearsal. This was my first full-on romantic lead. I needed to keep my head in the game. I couldn't allow myself to go to the places I imagined a conversation with my birth mother would take me.

I got off the phone with my heart in my throat because I'd been wondering my whole life where this woman was and why she had abandoned me. I told Jada that I didn't know what to do.

What Jada did was announce to the crew, "No more rehearsal today. That's a wrap for the day!" It was eleven a.m., but she called it a day, saying to me, "You got to go home and deal with that, baby." That was when we became real friends.

I went back to my hotel and cried tears of joy and sadness. I gave a good thinking-through and decided I wasn't ready to speak to my birth mother. That would wait. For me, the movie came first. I told my mom that I needed to deal with my birth mother on my schedule, not hers. Which I did, eventually. When I finally met my birth mother, it was neither as emotionally difficult nor as happy nor as sad as I had hoped or feared. I knew she was not the person who raised me, but I was happy to connect with her, know about my biological family, and have her know me.

As for the film, the shoot went well. I really enjoyed getting to work with Jada, who is one of the hardest working women on this earth. LL Cool J and Dave Chappelle had small roles, and hanging with them was a great experience. I learned so much. It was a very collaborative experience.

But no movie is without its moments of crisis.

When Jada and I had talked about the script, I had told her I wasn't crazy about the ending. She had asked me if I could come up with a better one. Off the top of my head, I told her how I thought the movie should end. It was a moment, and I forgot all about it.

When we got to the end of the movie, it turns out the producers didn't like the ending, either. There was a phone call to discuss it with John Singleton (who was one of the movie's producers), Jada, and Michael De Luca (then president of New Line). We were all on the phone talking about it when Jada said, "Tommy has a better ending for the movie. Tommy, tell them the ending you told me."

I did. They loved it. Right then, on the phone, I rewrote the ending scene:

The last scene has Woo and Tim (my character) in a car, having stolen back my Corvette, when she hears a song on the radio. I stop the car and ask her to dance. Because my character had missed his opportunity earlier in the movie, he's not going to hold back now. And then they kiss. And then a truck comes by and totals the car. Woo says, "I hope you have insurance," and Tim doesn't answer. Then as we go to credits, we hear Woo say: "You look better in a Porsche." Tim says, "Let's dance," and we see them dancing as the credits roll.

It really worked as an ending. On paper.

In shooting the scene, something did happen on *Woo* that put my and Jada's friendship to the test, and almost got me in a fight with Will Smith.

Although I had discussed with the producers Michael and Beth Hubbard that last scene in the movie, where I was supposed to kiss Jada, I hadn't discussed it with Jada.

I didn't know this: You have to rehearse a kiss. You can't just spring it on your costar. You have to work it out with the director, and both of you have to agree that this is how it's going to go down. All that can occur in rehearsal.

But we never had that rehearsal because we were over budget. There was great pressure to finish up and get the last shot in as few takes as possible. The producers said no rehearsal would keep things fresh and spontaneous.

I bought into the notion that "spontaneous" would translate into looking "real." And I didn't think it was all that big of a deal. I was young and inexperienced in making films, and although I should have known better, I didn't. I thought it was all good.

By the time Jada was on the set, there was no time to talk first. I assumed she was on the same page as me (literally and metaphorically). I was thinking, "Okay, I'm just going to go for the kiss."

However, when I went for the kiss, Jada tightened up. I did what I could to cover that up, and today, if you watch the scene, it looks fine. It's somewhat tentative at first, but it gets where it needs to go. Still, the moment the director yelled, "Cut," it was clear that Jada was not happy with how that went down.

A little later, Will Smith, who was on the set, came to my trailer and said, "I didn't appreciate that." I wasn't sure what he was talking about.

Jada followed him into my trailer, saying, "Will . . ."

But with my crazy ass, the part of me that I can't control, I said: "Go ahead, say it. Spit it out!" I was writing a check that my ass couldn't cash. Because Will is, like, six-two and, like, two hundred pounds. I was five-eight and some 120 pounds dripping wet.

Which is when Will went all gangsta on me, saying what I did was not cool.

Honestly, to this day, I don't know why he was so mad at me. I have always assumed it was because of the kiss in that scene, but we never did talk about it.

I played innocent to deflect the drama. I pretended not to know what he was talking about and goaded him by saying, "What's the problem, man?"

There was a moment there when we might have come to blows. My reactive fight-or-flight instinct was triggered and I could have exploded.

Fortunately for me, Jada calmed Will down. He may be known as the Fresh Prince of Bel-Air to the public, but to me he was a straight-up nigga from Philly. And being a straight-up nigga from Washington, D.C., I knew what I was up against. And that would not have ended well. Instead, nothing more was said about it.

Today, looking back, I can honestly say that Will really had no reason to be so angry. But if it was that last scene and the kiss that set him off, I would like now to apologize. I get it and his being angry was totally justified. (Before *Woo* was finally released in 1998, Jada and Will got married, so she's billed as Jada Pinkett Smith in that role.)

My only defense is that I was set up and I did what I thought was best for the scene. But today I do understand fully that what I did was not what was best to do as a person and not best to do given that Jada was my friend. So, for that, too, I apologize.

Since then, I must add, Will and Jada have been nothing if not good to me. I did another film with Jada, Spike Lee's *Bamboozled* (more on that to come!), and Will and I have seen each other at kids' birthday parties and events. He has always been nothing but friendly to me. He and Jada have worked hard at being good people, supportive parents, caring people doing good in the world. I have nothing but admiration for them and how they lead their lives.

Jada has always been an exceptional person. I remember one time, I believe it was while we were shooting *Bamboozled,* that I mentioned I was going to visit my aunt Alice—my mother's best friend who is African American and lives in the projects in New York. Jada asked if she could come and bring her son. She did and wasn't fazed at all because her background was like mine. I was impressed that she wanted him to see how black folk really live, and to never feel too far away from that.

And Jada's mother saved my life. She got me clean. More on that, later.

In the meantime, I kept busy with work. *Between Brothers* was a TV series I did that lasted for two abbreviated seasons (September 11, 1997, to January 29, 1998, on Fox; February 9 to March 2, 1999, on UPN). It was about four upwardly mobile African-American men who had homes in Phoenix and it told the stories of their lives, careers, and their friendship. It was a great show.

Kadeem Hardison was one of the stars. At the time, he thought he was a big star, maybe too big for this show (that happens). Dondré T. Whitfield, who'd been around since *The Cosby Show,* was a handsome lead actor who worked his ass off and was a great guy. Again, it didn't last long, but I'm glad it got on the air.

Pros and Cons was a very funny movie I was in with Larry Miller that came out in 1999. Larry Miller, who is a killer comic, knew me from the Comedy Store and came to me about being in the film, which he wrote.

Miller played Ben Babbitt, an accountant who was set up and sentenced to prison, where he teamed up with me. My character (Ron Carter) promised to show him the ropes, but he was actually just as clueless. Through a series of mistakes, Babbitt became the most feared person there. The prison kingpin, an actual scary guy, wanted Babbitt to use the prison computer to access his finances. Our characters managed to get out of prison by telling the kingpin he had some money waiting on him, and there really wasn't. Once we're out, all his gang came for us.

One of the funniest exchanges in the movie was between Larry and me:

"You know, hey. You know, I know how to be a gangster, you know?" Larry's character said.

"Man, stop that bullshit, man. You're in jail, now, man.
You got to listen to everything I say," my character said.

"Man, I could just go over there, man, and say, 'I'm
Shane, man.'"

"Motherfucking *Shane*? These motherfuckers don't
know who Shane is. I don't know who Shane is. You can't
use Shane."

That's the brilliance of Larry Miller's humor: "You can't
use Shane."

Pros and Cons was a fun movie to make, and it's fun to
watch, but it didn't score at the box office.

Malcolm & Eddie was another sitcom I guest-starred
on. Malcolm-Jamal Warner played Malcolm McGee, and
Eddie Griffin played Eddie Sherman. It was a great series
that ran for five years. On the show, I played Eddie's cousin,
Dexter Sherman, a quirky little dude who had lots of girls.
He never had money, and was always borrowing money
from his cousin, which caused problems with Malcolm.

The setup for the show was that Eddie was a fast-talking
one-man tow truck business operator in Kansas City. He
and Malcolm had bought their building, which housed
their apartment and a bar downstairs, which they named
McGee's. It was where the series' characters hung out.

I already knew Eddie from the comedy clubs. He was a
bad motherfucker. Came to L.A. from Kansas City, and
just lit this bitch on fire. Andrew Dice Clay took him on
the road and he became a big star. He got a sitcom and did
well for a time.

Eddie was doing well. But success can be such a bitch that it allows you to behave in ways that wreck that very success. Very few people handle that well. Eddie, like all of us, had his own issues. At the time I appeared on their show, Eddie and Malcolm weren't getting along that well. They had to have dressing rooms on separate sides of the show. These things happen.

What I will never forget from *Malcolm & Eddie* is that I knocked Eddie Griffin's front teeth out during the shoot. Yes, I did. And I am still sorry about that.

We were rehearsing. My character was an accident-prone, clumsy dude. When a bar brawl erupted, I swung my mug to hit someone else, and almost hit Eddie, who was supposed to duck.

Well, in rehearsal, he didn't duck, and the mug hit him right in the mouth. I thought he had popcorn in his mouth, because all this white shit popped out of his mouth—but it was his teeth!

Eddie looked up and his front teeth . . . they were gone, gone, gone. He was rushed out to his dressing room. I felt very, very bad. On top of that, we were scheduled to shoot that night.

I was in my dressing room, fucked up over this. *Think!* I told myself, *Think!* If ever I needed a higher power, that was it.

Then it struck me: I knew an expert dentist. He was one of my best friends. Thinking about a higher power made me think of him. He was one of my sponsors, my main sponsor in AA.

I called him and he said, "That can be done in three hours. Send him down here now."

It didn't even take that long. Soon enough, Eddie was back on the set.

Still, I was scared how Eddie was going to react. When he finally came to my dressing room, I was like, "Man, I'm so sorry." I had butterflies in my stomach. "You all right, man?"

"We cool," Eddie said. "It only took an hour. And I've been chewing tobacco and rubbing butter on my new teeth since then to match the old ones."

We both laughed over that. Eddie was a stand-up guy. At that moment, I thought, *Oh, he loves me.* And I loved him.

Chapter 12

Bamboozled

One day, my agent called me and said that Spike Lee wanted to come and see me. I said: "Spike wants to see me? What for?"

"He's going to be in L.A. He just wants to hang with you." I said okay.

Spike came to my house. For a whole day, he followed me around. He said: I want to see your day. So he did—not saying anything for hours, just sitting next to me in a car. Finally I said, "Spike, if you don't tell me, I won't know." That forced him to open up. I think he liked that I called him on his shit.

Spike told me he was making a new film. "There's a role in it and you're the only one who can play it." Spike then said, "If you do this, it'll be an experience you'll never forget."

I don't know if there's anything better you can say to an actor. I told him I would do any part to work with him. He told me I had the part.

A few weeks later, I was invited to New York to a table

read for his new film, *Bamboozled,* which was meant to be a takedown of network TV sitcoms.

Damon Wayans and Jada were there, and I was happy to see them both. I read some scenes with Jada, and that felt good, too. After the reading, I was officially cast in the film.

Spike is an introvert, a savant; he's super-duper nuclear intelligent. He's three people at once on the set: filmmaker, artist, hustler. I get along great with people like Spike. They get the many corners of my personality and I can speak to them in a language they understand.

For *Bamboozled,* I went a month early, stayed at Spike's house, and joined him in his research. We watched old cartoons, silents, and early film. I enjoyed every minute.

The cast was great and included Michael Rapaport and Savion Glover. Johnnie Cochran and Al Sharpton were also in the movie. It was the best movie I did as an actor.

Michael Rapaport is a total basketball guy. Loved hip-hop. We hit it off; to me, he was an NYC original. He was born in Manhattan and grew up there. He loved Eddie Murphy. He actually started out as a stand-up. He told me he used to dress like Eddie, in suits with all that jewelry. He was great.

Spike runs a good set. He is a consummate professional. And that's what I wanted to be. But I was struggling at holding it together and it began to show.

It was those aliens kidnapping me again. Being in New York, which is a twenty-four-hour party, where everything is available all the time, did not help. I was drinking and doing coke and I was fooling myself, thinking I could handle it and do the movie as well.

As shooting wore on, I was late to the set on occasion. Once, I didn't even show up.

That may seem to the reader like normal behavior for a

Hollywood star. But it wasn't professional. And it wasn't me. And it wasn't getting better. I couldn't stop those destructive behaviors, which I had convinced myself were necessary for me to function.

Finally my sponsor in New York said: "You got to tell Spike what's going on with you. He's been around a lot of people who have problems. His father was a jazz musician. If you don't tell him, he may tell you."

I had a frank conversation with Spike. I asked him to my trailer and told him what was going on.

He's a good dude. He told me: "I have selfish motives when it comes to you. I need you for this movie. I can't do this movie without you. That's my selfish motive. But secondly, Tommy, with what I went through with my dad, it's just going to destroy you. It's just going to kill you. It's about you and your life, your family and your career. So do whatever you need to do, in AA or whatever, in New York or L.A."

Then Spike said, "I want you to gather your strength. Who's closest to you?"

"My mom," I said.

"I'm going to fly her here tomorrow," Spike said. "It's the last week of the movie."

She was there on the set the next day, and she stayed with me all week. My mom was my rock. I started going to meetings again. Things started to turn around. I will always be grateful to Spike for the way he treated me, with respect, dignity, and compassion. He didn't judge me. He just wanted to help me. But I wasn't really ready yet to get the help I needed.

I enjoyed the time I spent with Spike. He invited me to his place in Martha's Vineyard. We had long, deep talks— talks about the way white artists are treated and the way black people are treated.

Spike would be all angry, and I would say that he was

being as unfair as the people he said were unfair to him. That didn't bother Spike. It did bother me.

But now, I understand it differently. Spike is an artist, and Spike is the sort of artist who needs to be in conflict with society. Conflict is what makes good drama; conflict is what makes great TV programs and is at the core of great films. Spike needs to be in conflict to harness that energy for his art. His anger is personal. It's not directed at any one person, but it is what fuels his way of being. It sparks his work. Back then, I didn't understand that.

As for *Bamboozled,* I believe with all my heart that *Bamboozled* is a seriously underrated and underappreciated movie. Perhaps blackface is too toxic a subject, but I believe blackface in *Bamboozled* should be looked on as no different than the Nazis in *The Producers.*

I won't say that it was racism that kept *Bamboozled* from getting its due. But I know that in Hollywood, like in much of the United States, there are only so many slots for African Americans.

You can't imagine the number of tremendously talented African-American women who did not have a singing career because Aretha had been anointed as enough. Or Jimi Hendrix as guitar God. Or why, until recently, you rarely saw more than one African American at a time being nominated for any acting awards. Terence Blanchard has written some beautiful movie scores, but he doesn't get the automatic nominations that Hans Zimmer or John Williams gets every year.

Spike had a moment in the spotlight, but then what? Is he supposed to take a backseat to make room for this year's acceptable African-American director? Why isn't he heralded as one of our greatest directors, regardless of race? Instead, he's had to fight for each movie he's made.

In any other country, he'd be one of their greatest film auteurs.

At the 2018 Oscars, when Spike Lee won the Academy Award for Best Adapted Screenplay for his brilliant *BlacKkKlansman,* I was on my feet shouting: "ABOUT TIME! FINALLY!!!"

Enough said. I've learned that I am not here to right the wrongs of this whole world. Nor do I need to carry the woes of the world on my shoulders. I am in this world and of this world, but my own mission is clear: I am here to do good work. That is what I can control.

Still, however much I thought I was in control during that time, I hadn't yet realized that I wasn't. And there were consequences.

I had lost my first family, having separated from Desiree, my first wife, because of my alcohol and cocaine use, and also because of her own problems. Despite our issues, Desiree was, above all, a great mother. We had a son, Jelani, and then a daughter, Jillian. I was raising Jessica, whom she had from a previous relationship, as our daughter.

After I broke up with Desiree, I was in a serious relationship with Arleen, who was a very unique and special person. When she moved in with me in L.A., she had two children, Alyssa and Anthony. We lived together for eight years. We had a child, Isaiah, who's now a young man. This special woman added stability to my house.

I was just trying to keep it together. It became a bad relationship, or a relationship during the bad times I was going through. That relationship, too, was chaotic and fell apart. Same problem, same result: cocaine and alcohol. There was addiction all over it.

But we have three beautiful children from that relationship and I am grateful to have them in my life. Throughout it all, true to who I am, and where I came from, they were all my children and I did my best to raise them and take care of them.

I also had a daughter from a brief relationship with Genevieve that gave us my youngest child—our daughter, Cameron, whose place in our family is just priceless. Everyone just loves on her!

Truth is, I didn't do perfect sobriety. I would go back and forth—on and off—but eventually my second relationship ended and we went our separate ways. That was tough. You can't imagine what it's like to be in a house alone, and then discover a kid's toy. It just strikes you, deeply and painfully, what you've lost. That hurts. But these kids have become great people. You can't ask for much more than that.

I grew up in a neighborhood where cocaine and crack were sold. From the age of fourteen, I knew about cocaine. But I thought it was a silly thing. It was like throwing a match on gasoline. Who wants to be that revved up? As a teenager, I smoked weed, and we used to drink alcohol. But from eighteen on, I didn't drink or use. I was performing and I didn't want it to affect my performance.

But when I was twenty-seven, I was in New York, as I mentioned before at the China Club, and I decided I was going to have a wine cooler because I had never tasted one before. One wine cooler turned into a couple of them.

Then I ran into someone I knew from the projects, someone who sold cocaine back in the day. And he offered me some and I said: Why not? So I messed around with it. And when the movie was over, I said, "I'm not going to do that anymore." But I couldn't stop. I never did it at work, but after work . . .

My using just took on a life of its own. That's why they call it a "habit." It was a downward spiral where using led me to hang out with more and more dangerous people, and hanging out with those people made my using more and more dangerous.

I would need to score, and I would have to go up to people at Hollywood parties, or people who knew people to score. I was sneaking around to get what I needed.

I was dealing with dealers at all times of the night and in all parts of the city. It is a truth told by Dick Gregory, and repeated by Richard Pryor, that a black man can land in any city in America and buy drugs within a few hours.

My experience was that you could go to the worst part of any city and you can just ask anyone on the street: Where can I score? Or you head to a strip club. At strip clubs, there's always someone who knows. There is a whole justification system where you convince yourself why you are hanging out at these places or in these neighborhoods, when what's driving it is simple: You need more. You need to score.

The fact that I survived and didn't die is only because someone wanted good for me rather than bad. I'm no better than Philip Seymour Hoffman, Heath Ledger, Marilyn Monroe, or Jimi Hendrix—or any of the nameless people, in every city in this country, who overdose every day.

Addiction eventually undid all the good things I had done, all I had accomplished. It was getting to the point where it was dangerous to my health. Where I was going to die.

One night at a girlfriend's house, after ingesting who knows how much cocaine, I OD'd. They took me to the hospital with no clothes on, strapped to a gurney.

My aunt came and got me and walked me out of the hospital. And one of the nurses, an Indian woman, walked right up to me and said, "God saved you this time. Next time, he might not."

And I was right back at the girl's house the next day.

* * *

As a sober person, I often get asked: What was your lowest point? Truth is, I had several.

One of my lowest moments came in 2000 when I was chosen to host the national broadcast of the Halloween Parade in Greenwich Village with Susan Sarandon. By all rights, this was a moment that I should have been celebrating: me, a movie star, and more than forty thousand people in New York's Greenwich Village. That affirmed I was a celebrity. That affirmed my fame. That affirmed I was a household name in the US of A. But I could not appreciate any of that. It only made worse my feelings of worthlessness.

My mind had a great ability to tally up my shortcomings: My second attempt at being a family man was failing. My partner was on the way out the door. I felt gutted and soulless. I couldn't feel anything. I was at the height of my fame and, at the same time, feeling like I was at my lowest.

But I managed to sink even lower.

I continued to do stand-up and book gigs all over the country. But my performance was getting erratic. At first, I never did coke before a show. Then I started to do shows high on cocaine.

It was a high-wire act where I thought the audience didn't know or didn't care. I was filled with the rush and the high that tells you how smart, witty, and charming you are on cocaine. It whispers how you can just riff to your heart's content—like free-form jazz. And some nights, I did.

However, one night, in Miami, I went onstage high, and I froze. I stood there and I couldn't talk. Couldn't say a word. I started to mumble incoherently. Didn't take long before the audience, which, at first, hung in there trying to figure out where I was going, turned on me. They booed me off the stage.

I was so ashamed. I was always the professional. But this is what I had come to. I grabbed a bottle of vodka and started to drink.

A few hours later, my manager found me. I was passed out in the alley behind the club. I had been found as a baby in garbage and to garbage I had returned.

My manager was able to get me back to my hotel. He left me there in my room.

And when I say that he left me there, I mean he left me professionally as well. That was the straw that broke the camel's back for him. He told me I was in great danger. He begged me to get help.

I said: Good riddance.

I told myself that would never happen again. And for a few weeks, I managed to pull it together for a few gigs. I was shaky—far from being at the top of my game—but I was getting by.

If I had to pick one time when I truly hit rock bottom, I'd have to say it was in Philadelphia a few weeks later.

Philadelphia had always been good to me. One of my best concert films is *Illin' in Philly,* a Showtime special that was a huge DVD success for me. Philadelphia has a large African-American audience that loves to laugh, and they have been my greatest fans since the start of my career.

I was booked to perform before five thousand people that night in Philly. I went out onstage; I had gotten high. I convinced myself I needed to for this big a crowd. I was so out of my head, I have no idea to this day what I did or said. All I can say is that I was booed off that stage, too.

My own cousin, who'd come up to Philly to see me perform, called me out: "You're fucking up in front of the people that will go see you when no one else will."

That was the point right there: It became clear that I was going to die if I didn't recover.

And that was when in the middle of my lowest point, Jada had her mother, Adrienne Banfield-Jones, call me.

I am not revealing anything here that Adrienne and Jada have not discussed publicly. In fact, in a very brave and honest Mother's Day video, on her Facebook program *Red Table Talk*, they discussed that for most of Jada's childhood, her mom was a drug addict. When we spoke, she had gotten help and had been sober since 1991.

I wish I could tell you today, word for word, what she told me. But it was not so much what she said, but the feeling she imparted to me. She made me feel hope. She made me feel like I could get clean and stay sober. That it didn't have to be all on me. That there were people out there, people like her, who were ready, willing, and able to help. Because they had been where I was. And they were now where I wanted to be.

It was powerful. And it saved my life.

Chapter 13

Doing The Work

Over the years, I've had a lot of therapy. And over the course of my therapy, I've had many diagnoses and treatments. Diagnoses are just words that help you get a grip on what's going on. It helps you identify a problem that other people have also experienced. It's a way to put your problem in a box that others have found effective ways to deal with.

We all know people who have large personalities that prove problematic and who traffic in bad behaviors, but who are very successful in their professional and personal lives. (And you don't have to look much further than President Trump to see that.) But when those problems or behaviors keep you from functioning, and when you do those behaviors without pleasure, without joy, but rather out of compulsion, that's when you need to do the hard work.

Over the years, I've been diagnosed as suffering from PTSD as a result of the injuries I received as an infant. When my mom found me in the garbage pile, I had been bruised and battered. I also had PTSD from being abandoned as a child by my birth mother. It took me many, many years to realize the profound impact that had on me and on my behavior. It's why in certain situations my only response has been extreme survival—fight or flight. My choice has been to create conflict or try to appease people in ways that didn't best resolve a situation.

When I was a child, an older black male and an older white male abused me—events that I spent many years not acknowledging. Not to myself, not to others. And it had a deep impact on my relationships with women and the way I behaved toward them. I can say it happened, because it did. And because my saying it changes nothing, but it means everything to me, and to my sense of self.

I was diagnosed as a sex addict. The general public thinks sex addiction doesn't exist, because they say: Who doesn't like to have sex? Well, I tell you who: a sex addict. A sex addict is someone for whom sex is a compulsion, something they are compelled to do in ways that are dangerous, risky, and beyond the bounds of respect for the other party or self-respect. It is a compulsion as much as a gambling addiction. It's a fever grip that makes one feel empty and worthless.

All told, I went to about eight different rehabs over an eleven-year period, until I found my place in a men's Monday-night meeting. AA is anonymous, and it has great power because of that, and I would never do anything that compromised the anonymity of any person currently attending or living sober. However, I do want to give a shout-out to someone who is no longer with us who deserves to be known for the lives he saved, including mine.

That person is Doug Fieger. Fieger was a very talented singer-songwriter, who with his band, the Knack, had the bad luck of becoming too successful, too fast. It all stemmed from one hit single, "My Sharona," and one album, *Get the Knack*. It was so huge, it sent him and his band around the world. At the same time, though, it made them hated and mocked. It was a moment of fame so great, he would never match it or reclaim it. If any people out there even know Doug Fieger's name, they think of him as a one-hit wonder and a failure. But the truth is, Fieger's much more important talent, and the job he did for more than twenty years, until his death from cancer in 2010, was saving lives.

It was in a conversation with Doug that I finally realized what alcoholism is. I never could really understand it. Certainly, it is a mental illness and a spiritual sickness. Doug was watching me go in and out of sobriety and it was going to kill me.

Doug pulled me to the side after a meeting and said, "If you die, I'm not going to go to your funeral." In my mind, I said, *Motherfucka, you're not invited.*

But then I thought, *Holy shit! It's my funeral. I made it happen. It's all me—my mind, my mentality.* It was me that needed to be treated, and once I understood that, that conversation with Doug was the key to my recovery.

What I had failed to appreciate was the physical, spiritual, and mental dimension of my addictions. The physical part—that was easy to fix in thirty days. However, the spiritual and mental part is something that you have to do every day. Treating all three helped me complete the triangle. I could finally get sober.

It's been a process, but I made the commitment. I knew that I had to work this shit out. And I have done the work. And it's paid off.

I realize that I can't control destiny, but I can do my best every day. I don't always succeed, but that's what I try to do. And that has yielded results, too, professionally and personally.

I'm glad I have a chance to talk about this, because I spent years working on my recovery. I've found that there's a connection with everyone who develops behaviors that are not good for them. More often than not, you can trace it back to something that affected them that is their core issue. It's always there, waiting for you. And when you meet it face-on in recovery, the work is hard, but the results are transformative, and worth it.

During this journey, I did reconnect with my birth mother, Tommie Gene, in 1998. She was living in Milwaukee, Wisconsin, and I was flying in to perform there. I invited her and her family to my show and they agreed to meet me at the airport.

Seeing this small, strong black woman who had given birth to me, surrounded by young men and women I would learn were my brothers, sisters, and half siblings, along with their children, was an out-of-body experience. We hugged instinctively and held each other tight for a few moments.

As is most often the case with adopted children meeting their birth mother, I was curious, but I found it difficult to really forgive her or to acknowledge her as my mother. My mother was Barbara Davidson, the woman who raised me and cared for me.

Still, it was an incredibly meaningful encounter for me. I learned a lot of my family history that I wouldn't have otherwise known.

My father was a much older married man who ran a funeral home. He kept her on the side. She was nineteen when she had her first child, my brother Raymond, who was nine when I was born, and she had two other daughters, who were five and seven, at the time.

I learned about my birth mother's parents: My maternal grandfather was full Choctaw Native American, and my maternal grandmother was half Choctaw and half African American.

Now, when my adoptive parents, Larry and Barbara Davidson, first went to Greenville, my birth mother was doing all right. She worked alongside them, doing the voter registration work. However, by the time they returned a few years later, she was already an addict and had abandoned me. I don't know the exact details of what happened in between.

What my birth mother said was, *"It was too much for me. I already had three children, he was a fourth one. I couldn't cope, I was strung out. I just left you and didn't look back."*

Raymond actually remembered me as a baby. It was Raymond who initiated contact with me and organized our reunion. Raymond is my brother, and we continue to have a relationship to this day.

It was Raymond who truly functions as the head of the family, who told me that in Greenville during that time, they were like wild children living in this abandoned house and in the street. And the only reason they were alive is that at some point he was begging for food and an old woman saw him. She asked him where his mother was. He told her he didn't know. She followed him to the house and he showed her the other kids, and she took care of all of them for a while. That is, until Tommie Gene came back in the picture and then took all the kids to Detroit.

Whether I was missing or had disappeared, whether I was alive or dead, this was not something she could deal with. It was her private shame. And I can't say she ever fully took responsibility.

But she did turn her life around. She became a minister, and she travels around the country giving sermons. And that, too, was a lesson for me.

At one point in my recovery process, I was at a residential facility and I asked Tommie Gene to come there. She did and we had an intense conversation.

She had said that I was a tough baby and was full of sores and always crying. She spoke as if that was my fault. And she said that Barbara had stolen me from her, and that she was glad to have me back. I confronted her on that and really laid into her on that.

And she broke down, just had almost convulsions of crying, of remorse and regret. It was like she was expressing the pain she felt about abandoning me. She said that she had lived her life till then as if she was the worst person on earth. And since then, she had lived her life trying to be better.

I was able to forgive her. Because I realized that she didn't abandon me on purpose. She had no control over what she was doing.

What I learned was that a person can do the most awful thing imaginable—abandon her child—and still heal herself. To me, that shows a power greater than reason, a grace that cannot be explained. I now understand how the members of that church in North Carolina could forgive the racist who murdered their family members and congregants, or how a mother can visit the person on death row who murdered her child. Forgiveness can be powerful. There are some things that are bigger and more powerful than ourselves.

I really have two core issues: That is like having Mike Tyson on one shoulder, and Jake LaMotta on the other. One is the abuse I endured as an infant. The other has to do with my being an African-American child in a white family, living in a predominantly black community.

I don't want to say, in any way, that I experienced any trauma because of my family, who did nothing but shower me with love. The trauma was from how society treated me. It comes from the way of the world.

The safe haven that was my family ended up causing painful situations for me. All the black kids didn't think that I was really black, because I had a white mom. And all the white kids definitely didn't think that I was as good as them, because I was black. It made me very sensitive to racial issues, to the point where they could be triggers for me.

Of course, this is difficult stuff to explain on paper. It took many years of therapy for me to understand this. The deeper truth of this eluded me for so long because there was an unreachable place inside me. It took me a long time to be able to go there.

I am not saying that being a black child in a white family is why I drank or took drugs to excess, why I got in fights, or didn't stand up for myself when perhaps I should have. What I am saying is that it wasn't until I recognized this issue, that I could really gain self-knowledge.

The good that came out of this understanding is most reflected in my comedy, because little did I know, I'm a crossover act by natural circumstances. I'm neither completely urban nor white, not just a guy who delivers jokes or an impressionist, not simply a storyteller. Instead, I am all of that and my comedy grew out of who I am.

I perform for white audiences, half-white audiences, Hispanic audiences, black audiences, Asian audiences. And my comedy works because it comes from observing them. I'm able to take a little something from everyone: from East Indians, from Spanish-speaking people, from gay people, from older white women, from younger white women, from brothers in the hood, educated brothers, from Jews, Catholics, Muslims, Hindus, and Buddhists. I can be 100 percent funny without being offensive, but still being raw.

I'm no Eddie Murphy, Chris Rock, Sinbad, or Richard Pryor. What they do is great.

But what I do is *me*. They can't do that. Only I can.

Because I have the opportunity in this book to do so, I want to talk a little bit about doing charity work. I am not the guy on the front lines, marching and getting arrested. However, whenever I am called to perform at a charity event, I am there. Whether it's for Habitat for Humanity, which builds homes for the homeless, or the Make-A-Wish Foundation, I will perform. I go serve meals at the L.A. Mission.

When my friend Aaron Wiener told me about the charity he established, Sarcoma-Oma Foundation, named for his Oma (grandmother in German) Linda Noack Wiener, who died of a rare sarcoma cancer, I thought, *Let's do a comedy benefit.* We held it at the Laugh Factory. And I can't thank enough my fellow entertainers and comics who performed: Louie Anderson, Eric Blake, Jeremy Piven, D.L. Hughley, Earthquake, Bill Bellamy, Aida Rodriguez, Craig Robinson, and my brother from another mother, Martin Lawrence.

One of the charities I am most involved with is the OK Program, which is saving the lives of young African-American youth from gang and drug violence through mentorship programs with black police officers. Donald Northcross has run this charity for over forty years, and any connection I have or help I can give, I've got his back. I do what I can, how I can, as best I can.

Thanks to my great friend Kenny Hill, I've also had the privilege of entertaining the troops for some twenty-five years all over the world: in Korea (at the DMZ), Japan, Kyrgyzstan, Kuwait, Abu Dhabi, Djibouti, Jordan, and in war zones in Iraq, at Bagram Air Base and Kandahar International Airport in Afghanistan, and at Camp Phoenix,

Camp Alamo, and at the Central Command in Kabul. There is no more grateful audience than the troops and no greater privilege than to perform for them.

Through my charity work, I have had a chance to share my talents with people all over the globe, and to see how all of us are connected in ways that are human and humane. That is a benefit that is so priceless and underscores why I am so proud to do benefit work.

When I finally got sober, the world wasn't waiting for Tommy Davidson to return to leading-man status. There were no offers to star in *Iron Man* (as was offered to Robert Downey) or to direct *Hacksaw Ridge* (as happened for Mel Gibson). But I was fortunate to have managers during my career like Sinclair Jones and Melanie Young and attorneys like Nina Shaw and Errol Collier, who cared about me and didn't let me financially self-destruct. They said, "You don't want to be like Jackie Wilson." They advised me on saving my money and purchasing my first home.

Without them, I would have burned everything down. They were the ones who told me, "Don't buy a new car or anything new for the first three years of the series." They wouldn't even let me buy a new house, just one out of foreclosure that I could fix up over time.

I was destructive to myself, but they protected me from myself financially. I can't thank them enough. They helped make my life and that of my children possible, more than they will ever know.

I was also incredibly fortunate that there were people out there who knew my talent and found ways to put it to use.

When I most needed it, Ralph Farquhar, the writer and producer of such shows as *Married With Children* and *Moesha*, who was a big fan of mine, offered me voice work on *The Proud Family*.

*　*　*

I am sure that if you are reading this book, you already know *The Proud Family*, but just in case you don't, it was an animated sitcom about a black family that ran on the Disney Channel from September 15, 2001, to August 19, 2005.

The Proud Family centered around Penny Proud, a four-teen-year-old African-American girl who is dealing with being a teenager, with Oscar and Trudy, her overprotective parents, infant twin siblings, BeBe and CeCe, and hipper-than-hip grandmother Suga Mama. The series also included Penny's friends, such as Dijonay and Zoey, and her archenemy, LaCienega Boulevardez.

It was a landmark series on many fronts, as the first-ever animated Disney program that was original to the Disney Channel, and the only Disney animated series, at that point, not produced by Disney Television Animation.

The Proud Family was produced by Jambalaya Studio, Bruce W. Smith's company. Bruce is one legendary brother. Smith, who was born in L.A., studied in the animation program at CalArts. He joined Walt Disney Studios to work on *Who Framed Roger Rabbit*. And soon after, producer Reginald Hudlin asked him to direct the animated film *Bébé's Kids*, which was based on Robin Harris's stand-up act. Robin, as you may recall, was the MC and impresario of the Comedy Act Theater.

Smith, who would go on to continued fame, worked in various creative roles on such animation classics as *The Princess and the Frog, Winnie the Pooh, Tangled Ever After* (a short subject), *Wreck-It Ralph,* and *Frozen*. Smith was also a big fan of mine.

Ralph and Bruce both said, "We want you to do the dad on the show."

I asked them: "What does he sound like?" They sent me the picture and said, "You tell us what he sounds like."

I did. And they said, "You got the part."

Penny was voiced by Kyla Pratt, Trudy (the mom) by Paula Jai Parker; Suga Mama by Jo Marie Payton.

As far as I was concerned, the dad was the best part of the show. He was a fall guy; he was Dennis the Menace. He was *Get Smart;* he was Fred Flintstone. He was Jackie Gleason in *The Honeymooners*. He was our guy, man. He was *the* guy. The show ran for fifty-two episodes, over four years. Everything I wanted to do with that character, I did. As Oscar said in one episode: "I can do anything a monkey and a nine-year-old can do."

Oscar got a lot of great lines. Like this exchange:

> *Oscar (to Penny when she wants to play boys' football): There's no pain like football pain.*
> *Trudy: Oh, yeah. What about childbirth?*
> *Oscar: Well, okay that's worst, but I'm not signing a permission slip for that, either.*

Or how about this?

> *Penny: Mommy, Daddy, can I go with my girls to go see the Hip-Hop Helicopter?*
> *Oscar: Nope.*
> *Penny: Why not, Daddy?*
> *Oscar: Cause I've seen that show and I know there will be boys there.*
> *Trudy: Oh, Oscar, you're impossible! Do you know there are boys at church, too?*
> *Oscar: Fine. She can't go there, either.*

Or this classic punch line:

> *Sunset: We need to respect our elders.*
> *Oscar: No, we need to bury them.*

The show won the hearts and minds of a whole generation of kids. How about the fact that the show's theme song, "Here Comes Penny Proud," was sung by Solange, featuring Destiny's Child? Yes, that's right. Beyoncé sang our theme song. She sang: "They'll make you scream/They'll make you wanna sing/It's a family thing." The song was a family thing, with Solange Knowles, Beyoncé's younger sister, singing lead on the song. In fact, if you go on YouTube, you can find Solange at a 2017 concert leading thousands of people in the audience in a "Here Comes Penny Proud" sing-along. And if that ain't culture-shaking impact, I don't know what is.

I loved that show so much. I did everything and anything for the show. They even used me when guest stars came in. And we had some great guest stars! Everyone who was anyone in Black World was on the show. In the "Don't Leave Home Without It" episode, Steve Harvey even lent his voice to the role of Penny's credit card! Other notable guest stars included Al Roker, Alicia Keys, Ashanti, Sam Jackson, Cicely Tyson, Anthony Anderson, Mo'Nique, Lou Rawls, Raven-Symoné, David Alan Grier, Jenifer Lewis, Mos Def, Vivica A. Fox, Ving Rhames, Vanessa L. Williams, and Cedric the Entertainer. Arsenio Hall provided the voice of Bobby Proud (Cedric the Entertainer's TV role) and the evil Dr. Carver in *The Proud Family Movie*.

Penny was a positive role model, teaching kids how to deal with problems they all faced, such as gossip, academic pressure, or dealing with your parents. Its heart was in the right place. It showed that families who love each other do fight. It stressed that money didn't guarantee happiness and that you should value whatever you have. It focused on what made for true friendship, and how family mattered.

Here's some more typical banter from the show:

> *Penny: Daddy, do you know where a the-saurus is?*
>
> *Oscar: No, but I know where a dino-saurus is. We call it Suga Mama. Ha, ha!*
>
> *Suga Mama: I heard that!*

One of my favorite episodes, "A One in a Million," aired originally on April 18, 2003. It had to do with Wizard Kelly (a Magic Johnson–type figure voiced by Aries Spears) and his famous half-court–shot competition. At each competition, one lucky person at the game got to choose between three basketball players and a friend or family member to do the shot for them. If he made the shot, there was a substantial money prize (used only for Wizard Kelly's enterprises, of course).

Naturally, Penny was the winner. Although Oscar had failed many, many times at the half-court shot, Penny chose him to shoot for her. No one believed Oscar could do it. But Oscar took his shot—and succeeded! Get back up and try again was one important lesson—not just to kids, but to the parents watching with them. More than once, it was important to me, too, to think of Oscar making that shot.

Take your shot. And if you fail, take it again.

After *The Proud Family* had been successful as a TV series (for a time, it was the number one animated show on the Disney Channel), Disney decided they wanted to do a movie. Everyone liked that idea. However, when it came time to make our deals, most of the cast expected that if the film was released in theaters, we would be paid the standard rates for voicing a feature-length animation movie. Disney saw this differently. They saw it as an extended version of our series for which we should be paid our series rate.

Disney's attitude was "Take it or we'll fire you." Instead, the whole cast quit.

Although I am always in favor of actors being paid fairly, I thought it was a mistake to walk away. I called everybody on a teleconference and said, "Guys, no, none of our black kids have a show on the air." It was true. At that time, *The Proud Family* was the only animated series about an African-American family, and it was a family that we could all be, well, proud of.

My pitch was simple: "Fuck Disney. I got that. But let's just do this for our viewers." And they said, "Okay."

We made the movie, and a whole season aired before they released the movie on August 19, 2005, on the Disney Channel, as the series finale. And the truth is, although making more money would have been nice, the money would be gone by now. But *The Proud Family Movie* remains.

Let me fast-forward to 2009 to another very fun animated film and animated series: *Black Dynamite*.

You may recall that during *In Living Color*'s last season, I developed a character named Sweet Tooth Jones, who lived his life like he was in a 1970s blaxploitation movie.

Michael Jai White was a friend of mine. And when it comes to martial arts, he was the real deal. Michael had studied karate since he was seven. By the time I met him, Michael held the rank of black belt in seven different styles of martial arts. Also, although *Black Panther* exploded in 2018, Michael played a black superhero in 1997's *Spawn*.

I had taken Sweet Tooth Jones and had a great script written around a character I now called Dragonfly Jones. I was going to play Dragonfly, and Michael would play my nemesis. Dimension Films was interested in hearing my pitch. So I flew my whole cast, including Michael and Carmen Electra, to New York on Tower Air, on my own dime. At Dimension, we had the cast read parts of the script and it went great in the room.

If you are not in the film business, you wouldn't know this . . . but most film executives spend the overwhelming majority of their days and their careers saying no. They only say yes to what they can't say no to, and the reasons they say yes are rarely about what is best or great.

So, when I got the call that Dimension was passing, I was disappointed, but not surprised. What surprised me was the reason they gave for saying no. Turned out they passed because they decided to do a different comedy spoof, a film called *Scary Movie,* which would be a monster success for . . . Keenen Ivory Wayans. And Dimension would cast Carmen Electra in that movie.

Many years later, in 2009, Michael Jai White told me he had written a project that was similar to Dragonfly Jones. In my version, Dragonfly lived in the present as if he's living in a blaxploitation film. In Michael's script, his lead character was a star of 1970s blaxploitation films whose brother was murdered, and he was now seeking revenge. The title of the script was *Black Dynamite.*

Michael said, "We're doing an independent film. We'd love you to play one of the pimps. You'd be great in this." I said, "Hell yeah." We shot on a VCR camera on a roof in an empty apartment building, and it got financed. We shot it in twenty days during the Christmas holiday of December 2008. It was grueling, but we got it done.

Released in 2009, *Black Dynamite* became an instant cult classic.

Two years later, it became an animated cartoon for

adults on cable TV, and was a very popular series, debuting in 2012, on the Cartoon Network's Adult Swim program block. I played Black Dynamite's sidekick, Cream Corn. In the movie, Cream Corn died, but he lived on in the series, although he did have dreams about having died.

Black Dynamite gave us the opportunity to go down some crazy wormholes. Check out this maniacal, clue-searching, crazy-ass dialogue we did:

> *Bullhorn: Man, you guys ain't had no waffles like these. These waffles are so good, they're like they come from down South. These buttery motherfuckers will melt in your mouth. Man, you ain't had no waffles . . .*
>
> *Black Dynamite: Wait! Bullhorn, what did you just say? You said, "melts in your mouth," Quick . . .*

That exchange set Black Dynamite on a tear: He erased the restaurant menu blackboard and started to make all these crazy connections: "melts in your mouth" led to M&Ms, which led to its manufacturer, Mars, the Roman God of War, which suggested the Greek God of War, Ares, which somehow led them to Aries and Zodiac signs created by Sahed in 785 B.C. 785 was the area code for Topeka, Kansas, and then they connect it to Aesculapius, the Greek Demigod of Medicine, and from there to Apollo. It was insane. It was crazy African-American intellectual paranoid genius. It was *Atlanta* before Donald Glover.

Black Dynamite once again gave me this whole new audience: a cult following of young, cool-ass, nerdy fans whose Super Bowl is Comic-Con. And because of *Black Dynamite,* I became a Comic-Con star.

You ever been to Comic-Con? It's a total fantasy world; that is, if you are a white teenage boy with disposable income. The giant entertainment companies prey upon those white boys. There are a few women at Comic-Con, and as many black people as capital letters in an e.e. cummings poem.

Chapter 14

Standing Up for Myself

Some people are really just one thing, even when they do other things. Jerry Seinfeld is a great example of this. He was a stand-up. He became an actor, who starred, wrote, and produced one of the most successful TV sitcoms in history. When that ended, he had made so much money that he never needed to work again. He married and had kids. He bought homes; he bought cars; he bought homes for his cars. He was interested in bees, so he made an animated movie about bees. He had a few ideas for game shows. They weren't successful.

If you were watching Jerry's life from the sidelines, as I was, you just thought he was adrift. Then Jerry seemed to make a profound realization: At his core, he's a comedian. Stand-up is what he does, that is his craft, and what he enjoys, and comedians are the people he enjoys being around and that he most wants to spend time with. That is who he is, and that is what he does. And from that realization came Jerry returning to doing stand-up, to his website that posts clips from his stand-up, and to his successful interview series, *Comedians in Cars Getting Coffee*.

Other people, like Jim Carrey, are more than one thing, and what that thing is changes with time. I'm more like Jim. Stand-up is not who I am. Stand-up doesn't define me. I'm not just a comic, nor am I just a comedy actor. I've done drama, romance, and reality. I sing and dance. I'm an entertainer. That's who I am.

But stand-up is what I do. It's what I've done since I first walked on that stage at the Penthouse. And it's what I still do most weekends all year, all over the country. Stand-up has given me not just a life but made me a living. And it is important to pay proper respect to that.

I'm often asked to describe my comedy, and my standard answer is to say that my comedy is like Bruce Lee's kung fu. It's a combination of styles deployed for whatever is needed at the moment. But as to my stand-up, I consider myself a working comedian. Other comedians are comedians for college-educated people; other comedians are comedians for an urban audience, or a redneck audience, or a Vegas audience. Some are cerebral comedians; some are physical.

Me? I'm a working comedian. I do comedy because it's the work I do, and I do it to entertain people who work for their livings and come to my show to be entertained.

My first televised comedy appearance was on the special *Robert Townsend and His Partners in Crime*. That was my big debut. Robert Townsend gave me my first break, and he and Keenen were co–executive producers of that sketch show.

When it was my turn to perform, I ran right out there onstage in this baggy purple sweater and white pants, which I must have thought looked good on me (what was I thinking?) and started right in with my Michael Jackson impression. I sang about how "I want the Elephant Man's bones." Then I did Al Jarreau and the faces he makes while singing, followed by Rick James at McDonald's and Prince, too. All of it was done in four minutes and forty seconds, which you can still find on YouTube, and which I promise will still make you laugh.

That's where Keenen met me, too. A lot of the writers and performers on that show would turn up on *In Living Color,* like Franklyn Ajaye. And because I was doing my own stand-up material, I was given a writing credit—also my first. I was lucky.

Once I was launched on *In Living Color*, I received an offer from Showtime to make my own TV comedy special. Showtime wanted to compete with HBO in the comedy space and produced a number of comedy specials featuring comics then, like Judy Tenuta, Elayne Boosler, Richard Jeni, even Jim Carrey. I made a two-special deal with them, with an option for a third.

When they shot comedy specials, they'd give the comic about $250,000 to shoot it, total. Most times, the comic would do his stand-up at the Improv or a local comedy club. They would shoot the comic standing at a microphone stand, with a brick wall behind him, and whatever money was left over went in the comic's pocket.

I didn't want to do that. I wanted my comedy specials to stand out, like Eddie Murphy's or Richard Pryor's. Sinclair Jones and I came up with a whole new business model and template for doing a special. What we decided to do was book a performance in a 1,500-seat theater, sell it out for three performances. That money would go in our pockets, and the $250,000 from Showtime we would use to cover the production costs of making a truly great special, including a filmed wraparound intro to the concert and great music for the intro, as well as when the credits rolled.

My first TV special was *Takin' It to D.C.* It was a half hour of stand-up comedy, and it was released in 1990. Produced by Paul Block, and directed by David Bergman, it was filmed at Lisner Auditorium at George Washington University.

The special opens up with two officers spotting me and giving chase as we run all around D.C., past the Lincoln and Jefferson Memorials, past George H. W. and Barbara Bush (impersonators) in front of the White House. When they finally catch me, they say that they're bringing me to my Showtime comedy special. They drop me off at the show and I run onstage.

For this performance, I'm wearing a loose yellow shirt with the kind of design pattern that would look right at home on the credits of *In Living Color,* baggy black pants, and all white-on-white mo-fucking Jordans. 'Cause if you taking it to D.C., you had better take it for real!

By then, I'm no longer looking like a goofy kid. I am now a handsome young man. There's some product in my hair, giving it the proper sheen, and I've got a handsome Billy Dee Williams mustache. And just the way I hold myself, you can tell that I've grown more confident.

I opened with some Marion Barry crack jokes, which, strange to say, still hold up. I did some of my old routines about growing up with roaches. I did some voices (like the Spanish neighbor), a riff about how when I grew up in the 1970s Sugar Bear was black. You can see that the audience was with me, every step of the way. I did physical stuff—like showing what a schoolyard fight was like—falling to the ground and going crazy. Did my Michael Jackson material, and it killed. I had them laughing in the aisles.

Man, I forgot I was doing dick jokes back then. But they were funny. Did some Anita Baker, Michael McDonald,

Lionel Ritchie, Al Jarreau. I was on a hot streak—and the audience knew it. You can still see it when you watch the special, even today. I had the whole audience clapping along.

Did a bit on *The Rastafarian Hillbillies,* as well as how singing the National Anthem has changed over the years and how a rapper might do the anthem. And then I was out. It was a tight set.

The next year, in 1991, we made *Illin' in Philly,* which was even better. It was directed by Keith Truesdell, with Sandy Chanley as line producer.

Philly was even better because it was in Philadelphia. *In Living Color* was hot, so for my intro wraparound, I got some great Philly talent to join me, including Jazzy Jeff, Charles Barkley, who was with the Sixers then, and Randall Cunningham, who was with the Eagles. They all took part.

In *Illin' in Philly,* you can tell I'm a little older. I've filled out. The opening sequence was in the spirit of *Fresh Prince.* No surprise, since I got DJ Jazzy Jeff to write the special's theme music with me (based on an Earth, Wind & Fire recording). The visual looks a lot like *In Living Color.* One of my best friends, Robb Armstrong, whose syndicated comic strip, *Jump Start,* appears in nearly 300 newspapers, helped with that. My hair was all edged up.

I'm showing how plugged-in I am to Philly: I had some fly girls dancing out front. I turned up on the court with the Sixers, with Charles Barkley, and on the football field with the Philadelphia Eagles. This wraparound was much more produced. I appeared in a variety of costumes, still very much in keeping with *In Living Color*'s hip-hop style.

When I got onstage this time, I was wearing a red-and-purple dashiki and yellow pants—actual pants rather than those baggy Hammer pants. Shot at the Shubert Theatre in

Philadelphia, I had more of an aggressive edge. It was a more profane show for an audience that is overwhelmingly black, in a city that is as black as D.C., if not more. It's to that audience that I riff about the differences between whites and blacks.

"We're different, but we're the same" was what I said. I did a whole sketch about how differently beer commercials were pitched to white audiences and black audiences. I talked about how Juicy Fruit commercials are X-rated. (Consider the words in the jingle: "Take a stick, pull it out, the taste is going to move you when you pop it in your mouth.") I did material about South Africa and how differently they protested over there. I riffed on horror movies and what a black Chucky *Child's Play* movie would be like (I sang "I Want to Stab You Up" to the tune of "I Wanna Sex You Up"). I got into how brothers last about 1.2 seconds in a *Friday the 13th* movie and in horror movies in general.

In this special, I did more acting, more characters. Much less running and dancing, although I did a few seconds of Stevie Wonder and I did Elton John. I explained that Elton wasn't singing the blues in "I Guess That's Why They Call It the Blues." Then I brought back my Al Green to close out the show. Some cute photos of me as a kid were shown over the credits. The closing music was by Chaka Khan.

Let me say that again: Chaka Khan, Chaka Khan. Chaka Khan did the closing music.

A couple of times I broke myself up. And there was more interaction with the audience. I got into it with them. Watching it now, I was definitely taking my comedy in a Richard Pryor direction.

It was wonderful, and it killed, and it was my best special to date. When it was released in DVD, it sold massively—and it was a source of some of the largest residual checks I've ever received.

I didn't make another special for five years. By that time, Showtime had stopped giving the same kind of budgets. Having done specials in D.C. and Philly, I wanted to do this in NYC. By then, I was back on *In Living Color* for the final season and I recruited Paul Miller, my favorite *In Living Color* director, to direct what we called *On the Strength in N.Y.C.*

We decided to shoot the special at a club, because Paul said, "You know, you've changed, and people need to push in a little bit closer to you." Given what I'd been through, Paul just thought it was more interesting for people to get to know me a little bit more intimately. And it worked.

In *On the Strength,* we took it to New York. I open to the camera, saying that a lot had changed for me personally and professionally, but what hadn't changed was strong comedy: *On the Strength.*

This time, I'm in a black sweatshirt and black pants. I sang a straight-up soul ballad on the streets of New York. My hair's closer cropped. The show was at the Bottom Line, a famous club in Greenwich Village (sadly, no longer there).

I get right in there, talking about brothers trying to get a cab in New York. I talked about the South. And the racism that's still fresh down there. I talked about how attached they are to their past. I said, "I go to a plantation museum. What's there for me?" I had a whole routine about white people square-dancing, which was just one line in my Philly show. I imitated all the instruments. I was a dancing fool in this one.

Black women, I told the audience, were psychic. They already knew what you're thinking before you do. They knew what was going to happen. They'll warn you, "Don't you be doing that . . ." They'll say that before you even knew what it was you were going to do. And if you said, "Do what?" They just said, "You know!" And they do know. They knew it before you.

By contrast, when white women get angry, they were very descriptive of their feelings. "This situation is absolutely incredulous," a white woman will tell her husband. "Did you see the way that doorman acted when he held the door for us. Well, I never . . ." And forty-five minutes later, she's still describing it.

I talked about the two types of white-male anger. Older whites make short statements, like: "You're out of line"; "Totally inappropriate"; "You're out of control." By contrast, college-age white guys can be mad at each other, but still be friends—friends but still mad. "Dude, did you really eat all my Cheetos?" And let me say, I am using this material in my act almost twenty-five years later.

They say that you learn more from failure than success. Here's what I've learned from my failures: Business is like the *Kama Sutra*. There are ten thousand ways to get fucked, and each one of them is different.

A few years later, my manager at the time, Barry Katz, who was my comedy guru, was going to produce my special for Comedy Central. I was psyched to be on Comedy Central, hoping it would be the start of a beautiful relationship.

Unfortunately, due to no fault of mine, Viacom rejected the special. Suddenly Comedy Central no longer wanted to be in business with me. After which, I parted ways with Barry Katz.

However, if I learned anything from the experience, it is

that there's no point in carrying around disappointment and anger. Holding on to that did nothing good for me.

But you know, shit comes round again. Last year, Barry Katz invited me on his podcast, *Industry Standard,* and we had an amazing conversation about my life and comedy. It was raw, and I'm glad that conversation is out there because we got really honest.

Another time that didn't go exactly as planned was Hugh Hefner's roast. I was never someone who hung out at the Playboy Mansion, but I did go there sometimes for events or parties. Hef knew who I was and would always say, "Hi, Tommy, thanks for coming."

When they were planning the roast, I got the call to come to New York to the Friars Club. Paul Miller was directing, so I knew it would be good. There were a bunch of comics there that I knew. Jimmy Kimmel was host, and the audience and roasters included Drew Carey, Dick Gregory, Alan King, Freddie Roman, Rob Schneider, Jeffrey Ross, Cedric the Entertainer, Gilbert Gottfried, Sarah Silverman, Ice-T, and Patty Hearst (of all people).

It was right after 9/11. Gilbert Gottfried announced he wanted to be "the first person to make a really-poor-taste joke about September eleventh."

This was the joke Gilbert told: "I have to leave early tonight. I have a flight to California. I can't get a direct flight. They said I have to stop at the Empire State Building first."

It was a room full of comics and the people who love comics. There was not a sound. It was like a tomb.

But here's why I love comics and why comedy is so amazing. That didn't stop Gilbert.

What he proceeded to do was to tell his version of the famous filthy joke, the Aristocrats. Gilbert's version, almost ten minutes long, might be the filthiest version of the

joke ever told. And the funniest. The audience was dou-
bled over in laughter, gasping for air. It was incredible.

Now, as to my bit, you'd think it would be mild in com-
parison. I decided to do Sammy. I came out and I'm swinging, and then I said: "You know, guys, this is appropriate
that we have this wonderful get-together in the Big Apple,
babe. In New York, New York. New York City, dig this. I
want to apologize for the Big Apple getting his two front
teeth knocked out."

And this time, everyone just fell down laughing. A joke
so bad, it's good. But, as you can well imagine, neither
Gilbert's joke nor mine made it on the air.

One person that I was proud to celebrate, not roast, was
a woman I believe to be one of the most important artists
of our time, and one of the greatest African Americans
who ever lived: Whoopi Goldberg.

Whoopi came to the set of *In Living Color* to do a guest
spot. My mom was there with my son, and my mom,
being who she is, and Whoopi, being who she is, became
really good friends. And so did we.

Whoopi Goldberg grew up in New York, in a housing
project near where the Wayanses lived. She first came to
attention with a one-woman show, *The Spook Show*,
which she performed in San Francisco and then at the
Dance Theater Workshop in the Chelsea section of New
York. It wasn't comedy and it wasn't drama. It was characters that Whoopi took on, making them real, and letting
us in on their humanity. It blew away everyone who saw
it, including Mike Nichols, who staged the show when it
moved to Broadway.

There is nothing Whoopi can't do, and little she hasn't
done well. She has starred, appeared in, and produced
movies, TV, comedy specials, talk shows. Of every genre

and type. She has been incredibly philanthropic, raising millions with Comedy Relief and donating to many, many worthy causes, including helping children, the homeless, those fighting substance abuse, and persons living with AIDs.

When Whoopi was going to be honored with the Mark Twain Prize, she called and said, "You got to be here." She called me one of her "Magnificent Seven," among them Jim Carrey, Billy Crystal, Robin Williams, Tom Hanks, Bruce Vilanche, Wanda Sykes . . . and me.

She had been concerned that such a celebration was too soon after September 11, but then she thought differently about it. "I realized that on behalf of all those folks I spent time with in New York, these things are important," she said. "We must pick ourselves up by our boot strings and laugh. We have to." Top of FormBottom of Form

It was an amazing evening. Among the performers were the "Queen of Salsa," Celia Cruz, Three Mo' Tenors (Victor Trent Cook, Rodrick Dixon, and Thomas Young), and a rainbow coalition of comedians. They were black and white, gay and straight, old and young. Among the comics, Wanda Sykes teased Whoopi for dating "the cousins" (white men). Alan King announced, "I'm the only one who knew Mark Twain." Bruce Vilanch, one of the funniest gay men alive, performed, and so did Cedric the Entertainer, Caroline Rhea, Chris Rock (on tape), Chris Tucker, and me. Not to mention Billy Crystal. And then there was Robin Williams, who showed up in a kilt and flashed the front row.

Stand-up is its own beast that you need to keep wrestling with, never getting too complacent. I believe I've only just really scratched the surface of my stand-up. Just the other night, after performing at the Main Room, a couple of lines came to me as I was looking in the mirror after splashing water on my face.

What if I said: "I remember being a black kid, and all the white guys saying to me, 'What is it with niggers and turtlenecks?' " And then in an English accent, I'd say, "Oh, I haven't contemplated that." Then I'd say, "What is it about white people and killing endangered species?" He'd say, "I haven't contemplated that."

I just kept thinking, *Jesus Christ, if that joke worked, that would be a motherfucker.* To be able to say that in front of an audience. Ain't that something, that *that* came out of *here*? It was right in the mirror, and it just came to me. If I ever could make that work, it would take my stand-up to a whole other level. Because stand-up is not like a band that goes on playing its greatest hits, you constantly have to adjust your material.

It all goes back to that Bruce Lee idea of training until it's a reflex. I am constantly adjusting my material as I move from stage to stage (literally, but also in my life) and as part of making natural the unnatural. I'm always trying out and adding new material.

Stand-up is like a muscle that you need to keep in shape. I'm still on the road most weekends, appearing at a comedy club near you.

I will always be grateful to Louie Anderson, the sweetest, most wonderful man, and one of the funniest comics ever. He was the first one to take me on the road and have me open for his audiences.

When *In Living Color* blew up, I would go for dates on the road and it was superstar shit.

You would go into a town and you were the talk of the town. Every girl was flirting with you, from the time you got on the plane, to the hotel desk reception, to the waitresses at the club. To a young man, it seemed like an endless buffet of pleasure, an affirmation of one's talent and ability to do no wrong, of one's invincibility.

There were years when I had tour managers or people who traveled with me, and then eventually I would resent them, or they would boss me. It just wasn't right for me. And the truth is, once I got sober, I had community wherever I went. In every city, no matter how large or how small, there was always a meeting and a group of people that I was happy to witness with.

I've done tours with other comics, good friends, like David Alan Grier, Shawn Wayans (who I've grown close to over the years) and Keenen—and I have to say that performing on the same bill with Keenen moves me because he has been so important to my career for so long and in so many ways—that whatever wrong I did and whatever hurt I felt are all past. What survives is our history and Keenen's talent which doesn't get the credit it deserves: He changed TV, he changed comedy, he provided a launching pad for this generation's greatest talents—and he definitely changed me and I was blessed to be one of them.

I've also had young talent open for me. I've been touring for the last several years with Eric Blake, who is one of the funniest, smartest people I know. He has a heart of gold, and he will make you laugh and keep you smiling for the next week as you try to remember what he said. If he's performing in your city, go see him. And if he's opening for me, then you are in for a night of some serious laughing.

Over the years, I've done a lot of late-night talk show appearances, and because I'm a trained performer, I always try to deliver for those few minutes in the chair.

Jimmy Fallon loves me. Because I'm *In Living Color* and he's *Saturday Night Live,* we're like guys who served in different units of the same army. Fallon just gets what I am, and what I can do. I remember him from the clubs when he was busting his ass. He's seen me perform, too. So when we ran into each other one night in a comedy club in New York, Fallon said to me, "Oh, I forgot about you. Dude, when are you in New York?" I went on, and he's invited me back, again and again.

Same thing with Leno. I was with him in the clubs way back when. When he was hosting *The Tonight Show*, Leno ran into me at an El Pollo Loco and said, "Hey, how you doing, man?" I said, "Everything is good, man, just, you know, out there on the road, doing what we do, you know?" Then Leno said, "You want to do the show?" I said, "Sure, I'll do the show."

Leno gave me probably the juiciest spot of the year, Christmas Eve. It was a night when everyone's home, everyone's watching. We did great numbers and Leno invited me back again.

I even got the opportunity to be a cohost of a talk show. Late into the run of *The Magic Hour*, Magic Johnson's attempt at a talk show on Fox, I was asked to come on to the program, first as his sidekick and then to cohost. We had a great time doing it. Magic had all the heart and the curiosity to host guests on his program, but, unlike basketball, it was not something he was practiced at. He just wasn't seasoned enough to be on the air that way. I had a great time and loved it, and would have loved the show to continue. But Magic had another path to follow, and he has grown so much as a person, and has succeeded so greatly as a businessman. Really, *The Magic Hour* not succeeding might have been the best thing that ever happened to him. Show business's loss has been Los Angeles's gain.

As for me, you name the show and I've done it. I've been on with Oprah on *Where Are They Now?* I appeared on Byron Allen's show, maybe almost a dozen times.

Beyond being a successful businessman, he's one of the
most beautiful people. I consider him a good friend, a
great friend. It's syndicated everywhere, now. I've been on
morning programs in every major city in this country. I
know what you can do with just a few minutes to light up
people's day. Which is why I keep getting invited back for
more.

Chapter 15

My Reality

People talk about the arc of their career or its progression. I have never really looked at it like that. Sinclair Jones had a plan for us that went comedy clubs, TV, then film, and we executed that. I headlined at clubs; I starred in a TV show; I starred and was featured in films. I'd done all that by 1991.

When you're young and hungry, and competitive as hell, it's all about getting to the top. And for a while, you can keep moving the bar up, setting new goals. Truth is, you need new goals, new ambitions to keep it interesting. But it's also true that it's so much harder to know what to do or how to be, once you've achieved your goals. When you're at the top, it seems like the only place to go from there is down.

This is what you can't know when you're young—what you can't understand until you're there—is that the only way forward is that you've got to change your way of thinking about your career.

Today, I think of my career, much like myself, as a work

in progress. I know what I know. I've learned what I've learned. But I know I still can learn more.

My wife, Amanda, is a big part of my current success. I met her at a comedy club. She was standing outside with another woman, a black woman, who turned to me and said, "Are you Tommy Davidson?" She told me that they couldn't get in because the club was sold out. I said, "If I do, will you introduce me to your friend?" She looked at her friend, and then looked at me, and said, "I will. I think she will really like you."

I brought them inside and sat with them at a table upstairs. Amanda told me she had a son. She showed me his picture. I got the impression from the way she cared for her son that she had her head screwed on right and was a solid person. We kept talking and took it from there. . . .

We were married on June 27, 2015. Our marriage is really a case of *1+1 = 5*. Amanda makes me better and more than I have ever been. Since we've been together, my life has changed for the better.

A funny thing happened in my career over the last few years. As I became more comfortable in my own skin, as I understood better who I was, I was increasingly asked to be myself. That is, I was requested to appear as myself on reality shows. They didn't want me to do improv, or do shtick, or act comically or dramatically. They just wanted me to be me. I had finally arrived at the place where, as my idol Sammy Davis Jr. sang, "I've Gotta Be Me."

I have a company called Tongue in Cheek, which sells accessories, ties, pocket squares, lapel boutonnieres. It's a very successful company. When I met Amanda, we went to Singapore, and I told her I wanted to start a clothing company. She said, "You should start a tie company first." And we did. We went on *The Wendy Williams Show* to talk about the line, and after our appearance, we sold out our entire inventory at that time. It's online at shoptongueincheek.com. Check it out.

In the midst of doing all these TV appearances, it became clear that people were responding to me on TV being me.

Soon enough, I had a great reality agent (until I had one, I didn't even know there were reality agents). She called me up with an offer to be on *Wife Swap* (a show where two different husbands or wives change places, being forced to live and cope with a living situation that's usually outside their comfort zone).

The agent said, "It would be real good, because everybody sees you as this funny guy. But there's more to you than that. You've lived life. You've raised a bunch of kids and sent them to college. You are stable, and a deep dude."

Corey Feldman was part of one of the other couples, so I ended up looking like the pope. Corey was so out there, but he and the other Corey (Corey Haim) were great friends of mine for a long time. Once upon a time, I used to hang out at their houses.

But you see, there was a difference: I got sober. They didn't. Which was sad because they were great kids.

I also did a celebrity edition of *Chopped*. Now, as you may recall, I was a cook for real. I worked at IHOP. I worked at the naval cafeteria. I worked at Solley's Deli. I know what I am doing in a kitchen. But being on the show was a whole other thing: They gave me a basket of stuff I had no idea what to do with, so that sank me.

But I kept being asked to appear on shows. One of my most fun appearances was on a celebrity edition of *Family Feud,* with my daughter Jillian, my nephew, my wife, and her sister. When I was a kid, my idols were the Jackson 5; now I had my own Davidson 5.

But, far and away, the best thing that happened to me was the show *Vacation Creation*.

One day, I received a call from my reality agent about hosting a travel show where they're looking for a host to take families around the world on luxury cruises to give them the vacation of a lifetime. It's *Vacation Creation*, she tells me, and it's a three-year contract—or rather a contract of one year, with two one-year-long options to renew (meaning that each year they can decide not to go ahead, but if they do, we've prenegotiated the new fee). It paid a good six figures. Was I interested? I was, but . . .

I told them I could only do it May to December.

They said, "Okay."

I told them, "I need more money."

They asked, how much? I told them a larger number. They said, "Okay."

This was the strangest negotiation I'd ever had in my whole career. It was crazy. So much so, I told them, "I just don't think I can do it. I'm trying to get movies done. I'm on the road. I just can't commit to six months out of the year."

Which was when I was told that the TV production and distribution executive for the show, who works with Carnival Cruise Lines, the show's sponsor, would like to talk to me. My phone rang, I answered. What I heard was:

"Hey, Tommy. This is David Doyle, of Litton Entertainment." Then he told me: "You probably don't remember me, man, but there used to be an open mic that you hosted down at the L.A. Cabaret Comedy Club."

That was true. I was the MC and hosted open mic back in 1988 and 1989. David said, "I was an open-mic'er, and every time I came there, you gave me a spot. And after I went up onstage, you often walked me to my car and gave me advice about my act. You put me onstage every single time. And I never forgot that."

He said, "I've watched your career grow. I can't think of a better person. I want this show for you." David promised, "If you do this show, I'll give you everything in that contract. And it'll be a first-class ride around the world. I will take care of you, like you took care of me."

How's that for some karma?

Vacation Creation was my main gig for three years. It's among the best things that have ever happened to me. I've been to Stonehenge, had a black couple married with a Celtic ceremony. Imagine that. I hosted a former fireman who was putting out a fire and went into a coma for six months. They didn't know what was wrong with him. He came out of his coma miraculously, but he had missed his daughter's graduation. I took him to Alaska, where he let a bald eagle go free into the wild. I redid his wedding vows, and he got to do the senior dance with his daughter.

I had a cop from Virginia who had gone blind in his left eye, and his right eye was going fast. His wife wrote a letter and said he'd always wanted to go to Alaska. I took his sons, African-American boys, one was about twenty, one was about fifteen, one was about nine. I took them all over Alaska: We dog-sledded. We went on glaciers. It was incredible. We flew in his street-beat partner. Gave him a certificate on the deck of the ship with the captain.

I took a married lesbian couple to Samoa. The day after they had gotten married, tragedy struck. One of them had a son from a previous relationship, and he was eating a piece of candy. He choked and died. We got the letter from them, and I took them to Samoa, and all over the Western Pacific. We spread his ashes on the sea and redid their wedding vows with the captain.

There was this little boy from Britain who's suffering from some rare disease. We took him and his brother all over Curaçao and South America. Dolly Parton sang him a song in front of the whole ship, in their very classic theater, on one of their top British ships.

I had a group of Mexican girls, four of them, that had a brother from West Covina, I think. Their father died suddenly. He was a wonderful dad, and we took them to the Panama Canal.

There was another group of five little girls that lived in the Valley. Their dad had muscular dystrophy all his life. He taught them to play musical instruments. He died suddenly. We took the girls all over the Caribbean, and we rode horseback. They performed for the ship, and it was great.

It's an incredible show. I got to meet these wonderful people whom I would otherwise not know, and I talk with them and accompany them as they have amazing experiences. This show not only helps the people who are on the show, but it sets a powerful example for anyone who watches the show, about compassion, about enduring adversity, about still being able to have transformative experiences.

My time with *Vacation Creation* ended in 2019 but it remains one of the best jobs I ever had. It's on ABC every Saturday morning. Watch it. I promise it will not only entertain you, but it will move you, inspire you, heal you, and fill you with gratitude.

I often get asked what advice I would give a young person who wants to be in the entertainment business. What I always say is: only do it if you really love it.

If you're getting in it for the money, for the prestige, or for the fame, those perks go up and down, day to day, and year to year. Someone's always going to be more famous than you, always have more prestige than you, make more money than you.

But love for something doesn't change, so love it. Love it so that you can love the whole process—all the ups and downs, the changes, and the twists and turns on the road. Love the process to know your career can be more varied than being hung up on doing just one thing, one way. My love of performing creates the space for me to act in any medium on any platform: to do comedy, drama, voice-overs, commercials, cartoons, or characters, host an open mic or a reality show. I'm not changing what I do; I'm just taking my talent into different and sometimes new arenas.

Regardless of what I do, how I do it is as a professional. It's Tommy Davidson knowing how to do a job well. Because I'm a worker. I'm from labor. I'm not from the artistic community. I'm part of the workforce. I'm able to do a great job. I did a great job at IHOP; I did a great job at the hospital. You hire me and you get a professional. That's the standard I try to live up to as best I can. Sometimes I don't succeed, but I try every day.

Sometimes I don't even have to get paid for it. With Magic Johnson, we had a Bible study group, where we'd always talk about things that were on our minds. I was saying money was a problem. He said, "Tommy, you'll never have to worry about money, ever. Because your God-given talent is always going to make sure to support you. Just like me and being a team leader in basketball." And he hasn't been wrong. Since I walked on that stage at the Penthouse, I've made my way, and I've taken care of those I needed to take care of.

Faith is a major part of my life. I'm not a religious person, but I'm a spiritual person. From the very beginning, with my foot sticking out of the trash, it wasn't me who put me there. And it wasn't me who made my mom see me there. There had to be a power greater than me.

Raising my kids is certainly one of the things I'm proudest of. I've been able to give them everything my mom gave me. I see it in them, even when they don't. They're so nice and kind and so cool to people. They're so giving and so loving. They're comfortable with anyone.

What raising my kids has taught me was that I didn't know any better growing up. I had to be taught how to behave. I had to be taught how to think; I had to be taught how to make decisions. I had to become a kid again to raise them, because I had to go back to age two, age three, age four, age five. I had to take what I was doing then, and relate to them as that kid that's learned those lessons at the age I am.

I would always start my conversation with my kids like, "You know I've been eight before, right?" I'd tell them all these stories about when I was eight. When that happened to me when I was eight; when what happened to you happened to me when I was eight, and this is what I did. That allowed them to talk about what they were experiencing, what they were going through. I listened. And I am so proud of them.

My proudest moment in this business was when I realized that I'm Barbara Davidson's youngest son, Tommy. When I realized that, everything came into balance.

Am I an actor? Am I the top actor at the box office? Am I the LeBron James of comedy? Am I gonna be a Grammy-winning dude? Am I Kanye West, or even Jamie Foxx? Am I Dwayne Johnson or Kevin Hart? Do I compare myself to what Jim Carrey has going on?

I don't anymore, because I can't control what other people are doing. I can watch them, enjoy them, appreciate

what they do, and learn from them, but I can't be them—
and they can't be me. I can only be me.

I have learned, the hard way, that a show business career where competition is king will suck the pleasure out
of doing what you love and will make the entertainment
business into a personal hell. When your comet comes,
you just have to be ready to ride the damn thing. And
when the comet passes, you just keep on keepin' on, doing
your work.

I loved my mother and she loved me. That didn't mean
we didn't get into it. My mother came to see me when I
was in rehab and we had us one epic confrontation ses-
sion.

It was more cathartic, I believe, for her than for me. She
told me things I never knew about how her mother had
committed suicide, but her father had told her that it had
happened because her mother was sleepwalking. After
that, she was afraid to fall asleep and tied herself to her
bed so she wouldn't sleepwalk. And how no one ever
talked about it. How she had been abused as a child. And
a terrible experience she'd had, being ordered by her father to drown magpies on their farm for their eggs, which
had made her an atheist.

She cried and told me that everything she'd been through,
raising me, and everything I'd been through, had made her
wake up. She repeated words I had once told her: "There's
something else in this world. Something that's bigger and
better than us."

When my mother passed away, I realized that I was her
greatest accomplishment. When she pulled me out from
behind that garbage pile, she did it on purpose. I remember her telling me that she took me home to the hotel
where she and Larry were staying. Barbara was always
bringing stray animals home, hurt horses. It was how the
Spence family lived. But when she told Larry that she

wanted to bring me home, he said, "No way. There's no way. Don't even think about it." He didn't think it would be possible. And he believed that she had no idea what she would be taking on in raising a black child. But she wouldn't take no for an answer.

My mom said: "I'm going to help this black child become a man and go out into the world, and give him a higher understanding to being of color. We will show the world that unequivocally, specifically and undeniably, love is in the center of every single color there is."

She set me on that path. She said, "I want you to accept that you can't change the system, but you can change yourself." She taught me that I was living in a world of color, and it was my mission to fill that world with as much love as I can.

I have. And I know that I will keep doing so. That is why I say that my greatest accomplishment is being Barbara Davidson's youngest son, Tommy Davidson.

Acknowledgments

It has taken me a lifetime to write this book and there are many people to thank:

Family come first: Beyond my immediate family, I want to thank my loving second mom Rosie Hooks and the entire Hooks family, including Robbie, Kevin, and Robert; my loving aunt Alice Fields and my entire NYC loving family, Willy, Scott, Joyce, Michael, Nancy, and Peter. The Spence clan: Grandfather Gerald and May Spence, my uncle Tom, cousin Shannon and Taylor Spence, my uncle Gerry and my cousins, Katie, Kipp, Carrie, and Kent. They took me into their hearts. And my for-always Amanda, who is my heart and my soul.

The major figures of my childhood: All of the children in Summit Hill, Rosemary Hills, and Glen Ross, who were molded by my side. My closest circle of friends: Tony Briscoe, Tony Smith, Keith Mayo, Spencer Moss, James Garnet, Kit Beckwith, Diane, Linda and Sonora Curtis. My teachers Mrs. Smith, Mrs. Perkins, Mr. Thomas, Mr. Dillingham, and Mr. Bombick. My supervisor at National Navy Medical Center, Joe Williams, as well as James Jones and "Stumpy." The major figures in my growing up: Howard Higdon and the entire Higdon family; Big Bill McMiller and the rest of the McMiller family for taking me in; Loretta and Marshall Hackney, along with Marc Baylor, Denise Baylor, and Brandon Baylor. Norman and

Rita Keating and the rest of the Keating family. Thanks also to Rosario Milian and the rest of the Milian family, Gerald and Glynis Albright and family, Chuckii Booker, Byron Miller, Emmanuel Bailey and Kitson Walker, for showing me a way up and out. Al Dale, Ron Green, Andy Evans, Ron Suel, Joe Gorham, Bunny, Sheryl and Eric Butler, Jeff Penn, Arch Campbell, and Donnie Simpson get respect for making Washington, D.C., my launch pad. Everyone at the Apollo Theater. If I survived when others didn't, it's thanks to all of you.

To the people who worked to launch me in the entertainment industry: Sinclair Jones, who had a vision for my talent and executed on it; entertainment industry professionals such as Suzanne de Passe, George Lucas, Jim Brown, Shelly Clark and Verdine White, Philip Bailey, Bill Hammond, Ramon Hervey, Iris Gordy, Peter Wise, Tom Joyner, Matt Sugarman, Brad Sanders, Nina Shaw, Cary Woods, Chris Zarpas, Michael Gruber, Andy Cohen, Stacy Mark, Errol Collier, Mark Burg, Melody Young and Jeff Gableson, Mitzi Shore, Stuart Ditzky, Larry Katz, and Heidi Feigin; Britney Buchanan and Monique Moss for getting the word out. These are the people responsible for setting my career on fire and keeping me from burning my house down. Without them, this book would not be possible.

Then there's my comedy army, all the incredible comics and performers I've been privileged to come up with, perform alongside, get to know, and call friends: Chris Rock, Martin Lawrence, Keenen Ivory Wayans, Damon Wayans, Shawn Wayans, and Kim Wayans, Sinbad, Michael Williams and the Comedy Act Theater, Robin Harris, Jackson Perdue, John Caponera, Dom Irrera, Jamie Masada at the Laugh Factory, Robert Townsend, Arsenio Hall, Eddie Murphy, Richard Pryor, Wendy Williams, Richard Lewis, Steve Oedekerk, Byron Allen, Bill Bellamy, Sommore, Paul Mooney, Finis Henderson, Sam Kinison, Andrew Dice Clay, and if my life has meaning and purpose, it is because I am able to acknowledge a higher power at work. The community I've discovered and built while in recovery has carried me past my highest highs and sustained me through my darkest nights.

I'm lucky. I'm blessed. I am grateful for every person mentioned above. I only hope I can matter to you as much as you've mattered to me.

Tom Teicholz is grateful for the deeply meaningful time spent with Tommy and thanks David Vigliano for first suggesting the project and Tom Flannery for fighting so hard (and so long!) for it. Tom thanks his wife, Amy, and daughter, Natasha, for filling his life and his writing with joy. Finally Tom would like to dedicate his contributions to this book to the memory of the late Sandy Frank, one of *In Living Color*'s original writers, nominated for an Emmy for writing on their first season. Sandy led Tom here.